WEALTH
WELL-MANAGED

MILLIONAIRE'S PATH
TO SYSTEMATIC TRADING

Escape the Cycle of Disappointing Returns,
Dive into Systematic Trading,
and Watch Your Wealth Grow.

ALEXEI RUDOMETKIN

Wealth Well-Managed

Disclaimer

ISBN: 979-8-89109-379-9 - paperback
ISBN: 979-8-89109-380-5 - ebook
ISBN: 979-8-89109-529-8 - hardcover

CONTENTS

To my dear wife, Alexandra
And my children, Anna and Nicole

ACKNOWLEDGEMENT

This book would not be possible without the support from my family. They are my guiding light and the sunshine in everything I do. Thank you for always supporting me. I love you deeply.

A very special thanks to Laurens Bensdorp who opened my eyes to the world of possibilities in systematic trading when I was ready to give up on trading. Without your books and the insights, I would've not been doing what I'm doing now. You've inspired me to not only be free from anxieties for trading but also just simply be a better person in a professional and an individual perspective. Thank you for showing a way and spreading the word. Now, I'm also doing the same for others.

A special thanks to Tom Basso for spending the time to read my manuscripts and providing me with a very valuable feedback to make this book better. It's hard to find an unbiased and a knowledgeable critic, who is also known as Mr. Serinity in the trading world. Tom did an outstanding job keeping me in check to deliver quality work. Thank you, Tom.

To our TMS Elite and Quantum Mastermind students, who volunteered to give me the original ideas for the book and later on to become my first readers. Your questions help you as much as they help me to be a better trader and a better individual. You make it possible for me to look forward to the next day to feel alive and fully charged up. You allow me to grow more than you will ever know.

Taking Responsibility For Improving Your Portfolio's Performance By Tom Basso

I've known Laurens Bensdorp and Alexei Rudometkin for quite some time. They've allowed me to beta test the software that they created for their students at the Trading Mastery School, and I have even been a guest speaker at one of the school's one-day get-togethers. Laurens and I share speaking responsibilities when we hold our Blueprint For Trading Success Seminars. So, I can safely say that knowing these two guys has changed some of the thoughts that I have on trading, which in turn has improved my performance over the years.

My recent best-selling book, The All-Weather Trader, details the progression over the five decades of my trading life and I attempt to describe my evolution as a trader over those years. Some of that evolution has come directly from Laurens and Alexei.

Self-responsibility is an important part of creating success in your trading. Even if you are busy and hand off managing your portfolio to some money manager or financial consultant, you are ultimately responsible for the performance. Having been a money manager myself for 28+ years, I can tell you that most investment clients don't think that way. Their belief is that "I gave Tom the money to manage, so he's responsible for my portfolio."

But, in the end, the investor is the ultimate decision-making on the portfolio. After all, every money management client had the right to cancel my contract as their money manager and move their assets to someone else or manage it themselves. The client hires me, and they can fire me.

So, self-responsibility is a great starting point to discuss why this book should be in your library if you are willing to take the self-responsibility for improving your portfolio's performance. The mental ups and downs that come with either managing your portfolio totally by yourself or hiring others to manage the day-to-day details are part of the equation and can harm your long-term performance if you don't deal with them. Firing a manager or abandoning a sound strategy in your portfolio and then moving on to the next thing may be nothing more than repeating mistakes over and over again.

As Alexei points out in this book, you can logically create multiple strategies that help to balance your portfolio's ability to deal with all sorts of different market conditions. Markets, and I don't just mean stock markets, all go up, down and sideways. Creating strategies or hiring managers that can exploit various conditions is a critical part of attacking risk, no matter what any particular market throws your way. Maybe strategy A is designed to kill it in a strong up market, but will, by design, struggle in a down market. Alexei gives you ideas and logic to designing other strategies that will slay it in down periods, helping you to design more balance and improved performance in your portfolio.

Sideways markets can cause many approaches to languish and can cause investors/traders to move on to new strategies. Why not look at strategies that, by design, should have an easier time producing a profit in sideways period? Alexei gives you the logic to get there.

All of this sounds great, but none of it will improve your portfolio's performance if you don't take the self-responsibility to buy, read, understand, and put into play the important ideas that Alexei covers in this book. Enjoy the read AND enjoy the ride!

PREFACE

Do you ever get this feeling, where it seems that the market is doing what it's doing, but somehow you are not "feeling" it?

You've tried to trade in the market using different approaches, and possibly even tried using different well-known strategies – and yet, it seems that it works only for a while and then stops.

You've fretted over your open positions, losing sleep at night, or maybe you've relied on your money manager to explain to you why you've lost just a little less than what the index did.

This has not sat well with you, and you are on a quest to find the solution.

Is there a solution though?

This is the exact question I've asked myself while going through the same pains mentioned above. Moreover, these are the questions that others have asked countless number of times and I won't claim to be the first or the last person to ask them.

In this book, I'll reveal the step-by-step approach for the solution to this problem.

You'll be amazed you didn't know that this approach existed, and even if you did, I'm sure you'll still be wowed at the simplicity and flexibility of what you can achieve.

So, read on, my friend – you won't regret it!

Why Would I Write This Book, And, More Importantly, Why Should You Read It?

You've made the right decision and decided to read this book, and the great news is, most likely, this book is definitely for you. But could it NOT be for you?

Let's see and clarify things right away. Nobody wants to waste their time on something that is clearly just... a waste of time!

- If you're looking for a *get-rich-quick* scheme – then this book is not for you. I won't promise you that using some mystery software or an indicator you can make 1000% in two days. There will be no big mysteries here, and no theoretical things either.
- If you don't believe in technical indicators and any of the voodoo associated with technical analysis – then maybe I can convince you this is one of the paths that can be taken.
- If you insist the stock market is only for the Wall Street professionals, hedge funds, money managers and the

like – then I can show you that you can *become your own hedge fund* if you like. You will have no bosses to report to and it's much easier to achieve than you think.

- If you think this is hard and requires a PhD degree, then I can assure you that you don't need to be Einstein to understand it and implement it. In this case, simplicity is the path to prosperity! So, all the examples, ideas, and concepts are for people just like you and me.

All the concepts and methods you'll see are what I and all of our TMS Elite students have used for years now. Who are these students, you might ask?

These TMS Elite students are the people who became a part of our movement to have a stress-free trading strategy for financial freedom. They came from all over the world and all kinds of different backgrounds and ideas for trading:

- These are busy professionals who think ahead of time and want to protect and multiply their wealth.
- These are doctors who try to work in their practices and trade stocks on the side.
- These are retirees who want to protect their well-earned wealth and pass it along to their loved ones.
- These are professional stock traders and money managers who were seeking to find a way to improve their performance for their customers.
- These are young and bright souls who dare not to give in to the overall mood of nay-sayers.

These are all people just like you, who were wondering and asking the same questions. These are the same people who were trying to find a solution and tried different strategies, but they couldn't see the consistency in their results. I have worked with them to show what is possible, the same way I'm going to show you later in this book.

Why Did I Write This Book?

With this out of the way, shall we now switch to the main topic at hand: *why did I write this book?*

A lot of people talk about the stock market. I keep hearing things like: "The stock market is down again, and my account is down," and "Inflation is so high, I don't know what's going to happen to my account."

And this kind of chatter never stops.

We get it on TV, we get it on the news, and in our social media feeds.

The funny thing is if you open old newspapers to some random date and look at the main headlines, you'll most likely see something about a financial crisis, which either just happened, was happening, or was about to happen.

These anxieties are what we're filled with every day if we try to stay on top of the news.

So, I was just like everyone else and did the same thing and paid attention to the news. I had money invested in mutual funds, in some managed accounts where a money manager was investing it into individual stocks, ETFs, and real estate investments. All of this was at the mercy of the financial news and once I started to drill down to it – the stock market.

For a long time, I thought this nebulous stock market was a very scary and intimidating place where only the elite professionals could make money, and only money managers at the bank had fully educated experience on how to handle my money correctly.

I used to come to my bank money manager for an annual or semi-annual review where he would put stacks and stacks of graphs and tables of numbers in front of me. He would talk the talk about why the market went down and why we might expect it to go up soon. He would also show me when the market went down, my account also went down, but not as much as the market did. He would tell me that this is such a good deal they were able to outperform the market!

I would listen to this and nod, but at the back of my mind I started thinking: *Is there any other way to protect my money when the market is going down? Why do I have to lose?*

As it happened, for me the tipping point was the year 2018, when at the end of the year I'd lost about 20% of my equity-related funds across my different managed accounts.

I told myself, *Enough is enough! I must try to figure it out.* So, I sent myself on a quest to see what professionals did and how they were doing it.

I read and I read – from timeless classics with Jessie Livermore, to more modern things like, "This is how you can pick stocks and make money."

Clearly, there was some very sound advice and some not so much.

I thought that I had grasped the old adages of "trade with the trend" or "cut your losses short but let your winners run." It all made sense, but one thing was nagging at me this whole time: *What do I need to do to make it happen?*

I started slowly and decided to follow what the books say and buy stocks based on this or that pattern, or a fundamental value, like PE ratio, or just watched videos of people claiming that they guarantee 90% win rate for such and such indicator.

I read more books and looked more and more at the market. I started to get a feel for how the market flows, how it goes up and down. I could see and feel that it's ever-present – but still outside of my reach.

Then, I came across a few more books on day trading and how one can clearly capitalize on that. That sounded very lucrative.

When I tried to day trade, I was literally trying to calm myself down before the market would open. I still remember the days when I'd turn on my charting software, which allowed me to place orders almost instantaneously, and then I would sit in my chair, sweating profusely, trying deep breathing to be ready for the opening bell.

I was dreading each day. Every time I placed an order and got into a position, I'd start the never-ending cycle of thoughts running through my head: *My God, did I do it at the right time? Did I consider all the things that I needed to know to place this order? Do I need to exit now or wait for this stock to go down?*

Each week the wave of relief was rolling in only at the end of each Friday.

This was clearly not fun.

So, I came back to read more classics. I tried then to see if I could read the patterns, such as head and shoulders, wedges, pennants, what have you. They would kind of work but then I would hit a streak of losses and I'd stop trading that pattern.

I'd try to day trade, then get way too scared and stop.

I'd try to swing trade (holding stocks for several days or weeks), then see huge swings in the equity for the position and stop again.

I was looking for a way to somehow make sense of it all where I could stop being stressed out about losses and not be tricked into opening positions because of fear of missing out.

This tug of war between different fears was so strong that I was on the verge of giving up this whole quest: let those money managers deal with it, they probably know more than I do!

This led me through countless hours of reading different books, to try things out, to understand different approaches to make money in the stock market, until I finally came across a book that changed my view of the matter upside down: *The 30-Minute Stock Trader* by **Laurens Bensdorp**

My Eureka moment came, and I hope I can show you as well why this was my Eureka moment and, I hope, you'll have it too!

I realized that I don't have to lose money and that I can be in control of my own funds. I can make money when the market is going up, down, or even sideways.

The approach to this is much simpler than everyone makes it sound.

There is no mystery on how to achieve it either and no need to be a genius to actually do it.

It is available to all who want to do it and my mission is to teach people all of the possibilities.

NOTES TO REMEMBER:

- It's easier than you think.
- Simplicity is the path to prosperity.
- Check out *30-Minute Stock Trader* by Laurens Bensdorp.

CHAPTER 1

What If We Use A
Buy-And-Hold Strategy?

The Stock Market At A Glance
Or Do You Want To Hold On To Your Pants?

Let's review what the market can do, but first, hold your horses. We need to establish some terms that we will use throughout the whole book, so it's better if you and I are using the same language. I promise you: it's not going to be a difficult language at all.

When a lot of people talk about the market, they immediately imagine the S&P 500 index. Or sometimes they talk about Dow Jones Industrials, and the tech-heavy index – Nasdaq-100. This is because these indexes are very common – the Dow and the S&P 500 date back all the way to even before the dreaded Depression and the market crash of 1929.

These indexes provide an overview of what to expect from the market within different time periods.

In this book, we will be looking at different performances of indexes, or stocks, or strategies (also known as systems). So, it's important to try to compare them as apples to apples and not apples to oranges.

Let's first introduce some terms that we can use to describe the performance:

- CAGR – Compounded Annual Growth Rate. We will use this term a lot in our discussions as it shows us how much, on average per year, we will get a return on an investment over time.

- Maximum Drawdown – Drawdown is what we will use to refer to the time when we're losing money. It's as simple as a percentage of the equity lost from the latest equity high. Obviously, Maximum Drawdown would be what was the biggest loss we ever experienced as a drawdown during the testing period we're working on. As an example, if we made $1MM and then we lost $200K, that means that we lost 20%, so our drawdown is 20%.

- Maximum Duration of the Drawdown – This will tell us not necessarily the deepest drawdown we've experienced, but how long was the longest drawdown. In essence, it tells us the time we were in a world of pain as we were losing our money and we were trying to make it back up.

And just to be sure you're fully interpreting all the graphs throughout the book, let me briefly demonstrate what the Drawdown is and how you can understand it on each chart:

Figure 1.1: Graph of a sample equity curve.

Notice how equity curve is changing over time. It can go up and then can go down. In this example a large drop is seen in the year 2022.

After the equity curve makes a new high, we can then measure how far it consequently goes down and measure the drop in percentage points instead of absolute dollars. This will become our drawdown chart.

Let me add the drawdowns curve to the same chart, which we will draw at the bottom, below the equity graph. Drawdowns are in percentages and are reflected in the scale on the right.

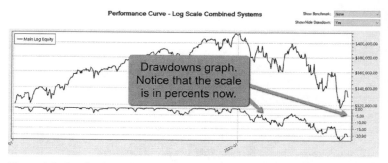

Figure 1.2: Graph of a sample equity curve and corresponding drawdowns.

With this out of the way, you should be able to see more clearly when we have all the graphs for our curves presented in the book.

Shall we see what the market, such as the S&P 500 index, can offer us from different times? Words are good, but visual graphs are so much better to look at!

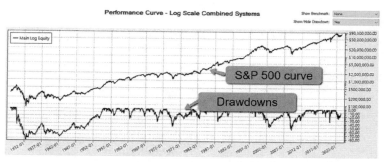

Figure 1.3: Performance curve of S&P 500 from 1928 till June 2023. Note these huge drawdowns at the bottom of the graph.

So here is something that people might not realize:

- CAGR is only 5.82% if you invested your money way back in 1928 and held it through all these years.

- Maximum Drawdown was 86.13% experienced back in 1932, even though the original market crash happened in 1929.
- Maximum Duration of the Drawdown was approximately 25 years!

Put yourself in that kind of situation now. You invested money in 1928. The market went up nicely for you and then... 1929 came and the market crashed and then crashed some more and did it for a few years in a row!

How would you feel if your money disappeared from you to almost nothing and then it took 25 years to recover?

Does it feel great or not so much?

A savvy investor might look at the graph above and say, "Yes, if you could turn back the clock and invest in 1932 and not in that fateful 1929, then it would feel like you made a lot of money by now."

Would it be fair to you, though, to think this way? First, how would you know that 1932 was the year of the bottom of the Depression? And second, how would you gauge that the economy was finally turning around?

The whole world was in ruins. It wasn't just the US that was in trouble – Britain, France, and Germany with its hyperinflation – they were all in trouble. Unemployment was very high, and people were looking for any job. Gold reserves were moving back and forth between countries and continents, as they were trying to fix all kinds of financial issues that were popping up non-stop. Small banks were going bust in the US while Feds were wrestling with keeping the economy going.

Does it all sound familiar? This kind of fear running through the minds of people is a never-ending cycle. Before 1929, there was an incredibly crazy euphoria and a rampant investment into anything that looked remotely investable. Even taxi drivers were experts at giving you a tip on which stocks to invest in. But, as always, it ended up with the crash – that was the 1929 crash.

That same history repeated itself, not in the identical way, but as a notion, time and time again.

See all those drawdowns on the Drawdown portion of the curve in Figure 1.3? That's right, those are euphoria times followed by a lot of fear – bull and bear markets! But you'll also notice that sometimes the market goes sideways too for some time, like in the 1968 – 1981 timeframe – the market went up and down, then up and down again. Inflation was very high and went above even 21% at some point (and we were complaining about 8% in 2022!).

So, how about we try to see what would happen if we were so lucky to predict that 1932 was the year to invest and we had the money to invest?

Take a look at this scenario of investing into the S&P 500 right in 1932:

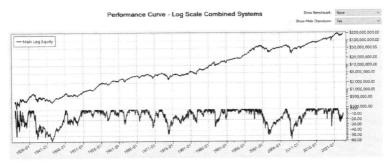

Figure 1.4: Performance curve of S&P 500 from June 1932 till June 2023.
Notice that there were still some huge drawdowns along the way.

This looks much better on the grand scheme of things and here
are the stats for that:

- CAGR: 7.89%
- Maximum Drawdown: 60.79% experienced in 1942
- Maximum Duration of the Drawdown: almost nine
  years

Are you still okay with the depth of the drawdowns and the
duration though?

I guess it's a tough pill to swallow.

It looks great on the big scale as shown above, but when you
put yourself into the "now," then it doesn't become all that
emotionless. Emotions are what we feel every day, and they rule
our world.

It's always so much simpler to look back in time and say, "Yes, that
was so smart to invest at that time!" But what did you actually
do? In the heat of the moment, we really rarely know what to
make of the ongoing events and how to better interpret them.

Relying on luck is not such a good idea either. Let me show you a few more scenarios where we just invest in the S&P 500 and hold it, and we will do it using different starting points.

How about if you look at the recent history instead of some long-ago era?

What if I pick almost the bottom of the market in 2009, which was the beginning of the longest bull market?

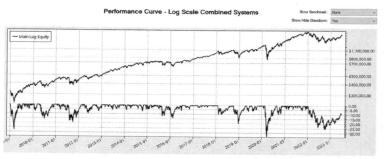

Figure 1.5: Performance curve of S&P 500 from 2009 till June 2023. The most recent drawdown experienced in 2022 is still the longest so far from that time.

Here are the stats for this:

- CAGR: 11.38% – now we're talking!
- Maximum Drawdown: 33.90%
- Maximum Duration of the Drawdown: 1.5 years and counting! We're still in it in June 2023!

At least we're finally at a double-digit compounded annual growth rate! This is great, and at this rate, we can double our money in about five-to-six years.

Although we still must suffer through all kinds of market conditions along the way and have no way of knowing if the market will drop again, like in 2008.

What if we picked it right at the top of the Dot Com Boom era, though?

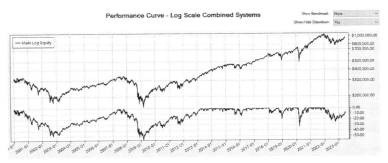

Figure 1.6: Performance curve of S&P 500 from 2000 till June 2023. There were some "fun" times to experience in that curve!

Here are the stats for this test:

- CAGR: 4.83%
- Maximum Drawdown: 56.61%
- Maximum Duration of the Drawdown: around seven years

Well, it's better than 1928 in the drawdowns, but the CAGR is just not as exciting as we would hope to get. We're not even breaking the double digits here!

What you most likely notice now is the timing of when to invest makes a big difference to your returns. Also, when we invest, we are at the mercy of what the market would do. **It can go up, down, or just stall sideways for a while**.

I don't want to bore you with the stats, but I want to make you understand what it means to invest in an Index Fund and passively hold it. This has been a very common topic in recent years, where big trading world celebrities all talk about passive funds as being the holy grail of investing for common folks.

One last thing we can review is the Nasdaq-100 index. It's the index for the hottest tech stocks and it provides the most compounded annual returns as compared to other common indexes we've talked about.

Here is the Nasdaq-100 index from 1995, where we can see how fast it went up during the Dot Com Boom and went down during the Dot Com Bust:

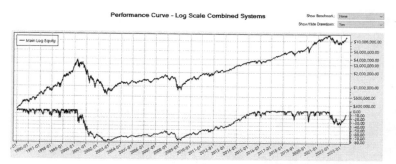

Figure 1.7: Performance curve of Nasdaq-100 *index from 1995 till June 2023.*

You'll most likely notice one very interesting detail here – there is a giant drawdown from 2000 till about mid-2015!

That's some index investing for you in a nutshell:

- CAGR: 13.59% – Nasdaq-100 does have double-digit performance, even with that giant drawdown.
- Maximum Drawdown: 82.90% – that's almost like 1929-1932 times for Dow Jones Industrials or S&P 500 indexes.
- Maximum Duration of the Drawdown: approximately 15.5 years

Again, this is not something you'd love to see and suffer through.

In a drawdown, 15.5 years is a very long time. The returns are great when you see it as a curve in the past, but living through that curve would have been definitely an entirely different endeavor.

LET'S SUMMARIZE THINGS FOR WHAT TO EXPECT FROM THE MARKET BUY-AND-HOLD STRATEGY:

- Depending on what time you start, you get different results.
- In general, over the long haul, unless you're investing in high-flying tech stocks in our current times, you will expect about 4-6% compounded annual returns.
- Your drawdowns will be horrendous. Expect 50-80% drawdowns and losing money along the way.
- Timing when to invest is very hard.

Should I Invest In Individual Stocks Then?

It's a good question. Warren Buffet is the legend of stock picking. So many people have tried to repeat what he did when he started his company, but it's much harder than it seems. Also, does it mean that we can avoid all these enormous drawdowns we saw with passive index buy-and-hold strategies?

Let me show you if we pick several currently known hot stocks: Apple (AAPL), Microsoft (MSFT), Amazon (AMZN), and NVIDIA (NVDA).

I've picked them because I currently know these companies have made a name for themselves and make up a very big portion of the S&P 500 index too because they are so good.

Here is Apple from 1995 till now:

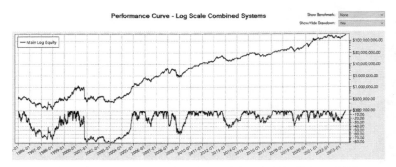

Figure 1.8: Performance curve of Apple stock from 1995 till June 2023.

Quick stats:

- CAGR: 24.76%
- Maximum Drawdown: 81.97%

- Maximum Duration of the Drawdown: around five years

This shows very good compounded annual returns, but would you really pick that stock way back in 1995? And the most important question: would you hold it through different bust cycles? Almost 82% of the drawdown is not for the faint of heart, and sitting in the longest drawdown for almost five years is not something most people would find appealing.

How about we see what Microsoft has to offer:

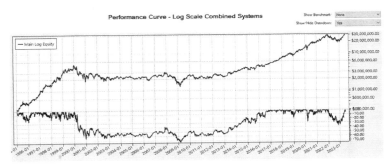

Figure 1.9: Performance of Microsoft stock from 1995 till June 2023.

Quick stats:

- CAGR: 17.09%
- Maximum Drawdown: 74.57%
- Maximum Duration of the Drawdown: around 17 years

Well, who would in their right mind hold this stock from 2000 till 2017? It did go down after the big rally of Dot Com Boom where it stayed for a long, long time.

How did Amazon do then?

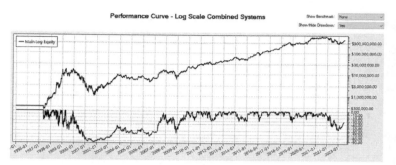

Figure 1.10: Performance of Amazon stock from 1995 till June 2023.

Quick stats:

- CAGR: 28.61%
- Maximum Drawdown: 94.42% – Oh yes, everyone wants to see that discouragingly huge kind of drawdown!
- Maximum Duration of the Drawdown: around ten years

Oh my, that compounded return is so good, but the drawdown! That's a little more than crazy now. It's like losing all your money and then somehow thinking you will get it all back.

How about NVIDIA stock? Keep in mind, this stock didn't even exist way back in 1995, so the graph looks a little bit different and flat at the beginning:

Figure 1.11: Performance of NVIDIA stock from 1995 till June 2023.

Quick stats:

- CAGR: 27.50%
- Maximum Drawdown: 90.22% – Same deep drawdowns here!
- Maximum Duration of the Drawdown: around 8.5 years

Can you just imagine for a second you've invested one million dollars in Amazon stock and then lost $944,200 of it in a couple of years? You were left with only $65,800, and hoping by some miracle that this would go back up to break even, let alone make you money.

Show me at least one person who can say, "Yes, I'm all for that! I believe in this stock so much that I'm okay to lose almost all of my investments, and I'll definitely make it back up some time in the future."

I guess I'm just not built that way; I can't be that person.

Investing in individual stocks seems to be lucrative from the performance perspective, but it's possible to incur much larger drawdowns than you'd expect from the indexes.

This is because indexes are made up of a blend of different stocks, and things are smoothed out. This also smooths out the returns along the way. This smoothing effect is why our drawdowns in the index are smaller than individual stocks, but our returns are not even double digits from the same time period.

If we try to create a blend of stocks that we choose, then we can end up with much larger returns than any individual stocks by themselves.

Take a look at this. We're blending Apple, Microsoft, Amazon, and NVIDIA at equal allocations. I threw in NVIDIA because it's been such a favorite stock lately due to all the hype with Artificial Intelligence:

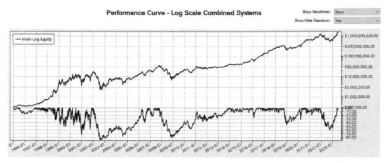

Figure 1.12: Performance curve of Apple, Microsoft, Amazon, and NVIDIA from 1995 till June 2023.

Quick stats:

- CAGR: 34.65%
- Maximum Drawdown: 88.16%
- Maximum Duration of the Drawdown: around six years

This does look better in terms of the performance and the maximum duration of the drawdown, but the drawdown is still very large.

Let's put things side by side for comparison:

	S&P 500 B&H*	AAPL Stock B&H*	MSFT Stock B&H*	AMZN Stock B&H*	NVDA Stock B&H*	Combined (AAPL, MSFT, AMZN, NVDA) B&H*
CAGR	8.27%	24.76%	17.09%	28.62%	27.50%	**34.65%**
Max Drawdown	56.58%	81.97%	74.57%	94.42%	90.22%	**88.16%**
Max Duration of the Drawdown	7.2 years	~5 years	17 years	~10 years	8.5 years	**6 years**

*B&H: Buy and Hold

Table 1.1: Various Buy-and-Hold instruments from 1995 till June 2023.

Did you notice one peculiar thing in the stats here though? Did you see that the combined CAGR is much larger than that of any individual stock or index?

Do you know why the CAGR for the combo is better?

We will be using this concept over and over in this book, so I wanted to make sure you saw that!

This concept is what is called a **non-correlated approach**. I want you to see it and realize it here, but we will go into more detail a little later. We will use this to our advantage as we will start working with systems and a suite of systems – but I'm getting ahead of myself.

Let's get back to the stocks above and what they can provide to us. As you saw, each stock can provide a very high CAGR, but it's usually accompanied by very large drawdowns.

I chose these stocks because I know they are the ones that are making a name for themselves in our current market conditions.

I chose these stocks with my recency bias at play.

What if I were wrong and next year they would go down, as they did in 2000?

What if the market turned down next year or some other year and these stocks would lose their value by 30-50-80%?

How could I know that?

I can't know that, and I don't need to know that. If I use a systematic approach to see which stocks to enter into and at what time – that's all I need to know.

USING INDIVIDUAL STOCKS FOR BUY AND HOLD:

- Recency bias could mislead you.
- Holding individual stocks can be very risky.
- Your drawdowns can be so bad that you might experience a total loss for any individual stock if the company goes bankrupt.
- The good news is that returns could be so much better than investing in indexes.

How About Blending Things Together?

Did you notice in the example above when we combined all of the stocks together and then gave them equal allocations, that the result was much better than that of any individual stock?

How come we've ended up with a CAGR of 34.65%, even though all of the stocks in question were below 30% CAGR?

Also, how come having NVIDIA and Amazon at more than 90% drawdowns we ended up with only 88% drawdown with the blend?

This is where the trick of "diversification" comes into play. In other words, when you create a blend of stocks and some are moving in one direction, while the others are moving in the opposite direction, then we can get an effect of one stock propping the other stock.

This is what we call a non-correlation behavior.

Bank managers love to use the term "diversification," but what they are trying to tell you is by diversifying they will invest in probably non-correlated stocks or assets. An example of that might be investing 60% in equities and 40% in bonds. For our purposes, we will only focus on the non-correlation between equity, or stocks.

Unfortunately, most stocks are quite correlated with each other. If the market is going up, then the greatest number of stocks is going up. If the market is going down, then the greatest number of stocks is going down.

The index itself is a blend of stocks, remember? It's a typical chicken or the egg problem here: who affects whom? Is it the fact that a market index is going down then most of the stocks are following it, or is it because individual stocks are going down, then the index is following the stocks?

In some cases, you can't really tell which one is which.

But we can use this knowledge to gauge what we can do when we're developing our systems.

BLENDING STOCKS FOR A BUY-AND-HOLD STRATEGY:

- You can increase your overall returns.
- You can reduce your risks.
- Non-correlation is what we're after for returns and risks.
- Indexes are also just a blend of individual stocks chosen by some rule.

CHAPTER 2

The Rules Are Great!

What Are The Rules And What Can We Do With Them?

Let me tell you what the students from our Elite mentoring program ask:

- Can I just use the buy-and-hold approach?
- How would I know when to exit and when to enter?
- How much do I need to invest in any stock?
- I've tried all kinds of systems and read a lot of different books, why can't I get consistent results?
- How can I make money in the bear market conditions?
- How can I avoid losing what I've made?
- Do I have to sit in front of the computer all day to trade stocks?
- Do I have to do everything manually?
- And many more questions like that...

The answers to this barrage of questions lie in returning to the basics. In Chapter 1, I illustrated the implications of employing a buy-and-hold strategy for an index, individual stocks, or even a blend of stocks.

What would it mean then to create a consistency of the results and figure out what to do at any given moment? Keywords to notice here are "create a consistency of the results."

I hope you guessed it – it's coming up with a set of specific rules to handle all these different conditions!

Rules will tell us: what stocks to work with, and when to enter a trade or when to exit; how much to buy and how much to sell; what to do if the market is bear or bull; how to let your winners run and cut your losses short – all of that is what rules will do for us.

Rules are what we will use to describe our strategy. We can call each set of rules our **System**.

A system will help us figure out which stock universe we will work with, the conditions we will use to enter a trade and to exit it, and how many shares to get for any given stock.

We can apply a set of buy-and-sell rules (a system) to an individual stock, an index, or a set of stocks. This will help us systematize what we are trying to achieve by crafting our rules.

Obviously, rules can't just appear from nowhere. We are going to use our ideas regarding what we want first, before coming up with what rules to use.

This is called: *idea first system creation.*

You define a set of objectives based on a general idea and then come up with a set of rules (conditions) to create your system.

It sounds complicated, but if you step back for a second and relate to an ordinary life task, then it becomes quite easy. I'll give you an example:

- You want to go to a restaurant, but the restaurant is ten miles away. You have a car in your garage. So, the first rule is: you need to have a car to drive to the restaurant.
- Who would be driving this car? You can then set rule number two: you'll be the driver.
- You'd need to make sure that there is enough gas, and the car can start. Rule number three: you pick up your keys and check the gas.

This seems simplistic, but isn't it what we do all the time? We don't think of it as rules, but rather we take it for granted; however, if we decipher things, then it comes down to a set of rules.

You could've just as easily chosen a different set of rules to get to the same restaurant and that would've been a completely different strategy. An example: you could call an Uber service to drive you there, or have your personal driver take you there.

In other words, having rules is what we do in our lives anyway, so we need to approach stock trading the same exact way if we want to have consistency and have answers to what to do and when.

A SET OF RULES IS YOUR SYSTEM, AKA STRATEGY:

- Stocks universe: which stock(s) to work with?
- Filters: is there any way to narrow that list down?
- Entries and exits: what conditions should trigger an entry or an exit?
- Sizing your positions: how many shares to buy or sell?

Let's Use Rules To Define A System

Using conditions to define a system is not difficult at all. The difficulty lies in trying to figure out if these rules make sense. That's why the easiest way to determine their effectiveness is to use backtesting.

Backtesting allows you to verify if the rules you've picked have at least some sense to them, and by sense we mean, let's assume the system makes money.

Let's conduct a small experiment and come up with a set of rules.

Here is an idea that we can use:

- We want to pick stocks to invest in, so we will be working with stocks.
- We want to ensure we get into stocks that are trending up on a longer-term basis.
- We want to stay with these stocks once we've picked them.

Using our "idea first" approach, we can come up with the following rules:

- The assumption is that the stocks that are moving up the most over the longer period of time have a good chance of continuing to go up.
- We can define that "period of time" as one trading year in our example – which translates into 252 trading days.
- That seems to be long enough to judge if the stock made money. Plus, what does it mean for a stock to "make money"? We can see how much that stock grew in value using a Rate of Change (ROC), which represents the percentage the stock grew in X days.

Now, what universe of stocks are we going to use for this rule? That can depend on which stocks you want to get into. For our example system, we will use Nasdaq-100 stocks because there are only 100 stocks in that index at any given time, and we know these are raving hot technology stocks in most cases. So, we should expect a lot of growth for these stocks.

Even though there are 100 stocks and not thousands available on the exchange, it's still a lot to deal with. So, we will try to pick only the first ten stocks with the highest rate of change in the last 252 days from the Nasdaq-100 index. The idea is to get the best of the best from that index and invest only in these top-performing stocks.

Here is our system so far:

- Stock universe: Nasdaq-100 with the historical joiners and leavers.

- Ranking: Highest Rate of Change over 252 days. Ranking is the process of sorting our candidates and then deciding which ones are the best candidates.
- We will enter ten positions at a time and keep these stocks.

What do you think would happen if we just hold these stocks?

Before we answer this question, if you look closely then you might notice our rules seem incomplete:

1) There is no indication of how much to buy to get into these positions.
2) There is no rule that tells us under what circumstances to exit from these stocks.

To address 1) above, we would need to think of an idea of what we can call **Position Sizing.** It tells us how much stock to buy at any given time.

There are all kinds of ways to calculate how much stock to buy, but in our example, we will use the simplest method: **percentage-based sizing.**

If we have 100% equity assigned to our system, we can allocate an equal amount of that equity across all ten positions, making it 10% per position. Simple, right?

We will then complement our system rules with the position sizing mentioned above.

Regarding 2) above: when do we exit from a position? But why do we need to know it?

The answer is simple too. If you don't employ any exit rules, then it's *a buy-and-hold strategy all over again*, but with rules just to choose your initial stocks.

This could be what you're looking for, and let me just show you what this produces starting from 1995:

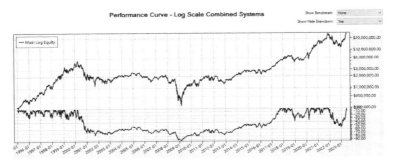

Figure 2.1: *Performance curve for* Nasdaq-100 *system where we buy and hold ten best stocks from 1995 to June 2023.*

And take a look at what trades it got into:

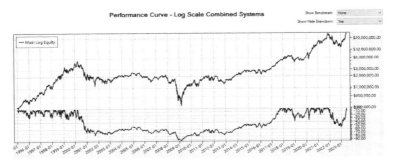

Figure 2.2: *Trades for the* Nasdaq-100 *system where we buy and hold ten best stocks from 1995 to June 2023.*

Way back in 1995, we got into some hot stocks at that time, but later some of them were delisted. So, we got into other stocks and have been holding them for a very long time.

As a sidenote, when a stock is delisted, your broker will most likely either sell the positions for you, or you'd need to sell these shares on the over-the-counter (OTC) market. In our example, we're assuming that if a stock is delisted, we'll close down the position and then look to open a new set of stocks to replace the ones that were delisted, all the while still following the same exact rules to open a new position.

At least with this system, we didn't have to choose which stocks to get and hold. System rules did it all for us!

Let's reiterate all the rules that we have for this system so far:

- Stock universe: Nasdaq-100 with the historical joiners and leavers
- Ranking: Highest Rate of Change over 252 days
- We will enter ten positions at a time and keep those stocks.
- We will use percent-based position sizing to allocate 10% of the total equity to each stock for our system.
- If a stock is delisted, then we will find a next candidate to get into a position.

Quick stats:

- CAGR: 16.58%
- Maximum Drawdown: 93.43%

- Maximum Duration of the Drawdown: around 17.5 years

The stats for this system are good (at least for the upside). Now, take a look at how it compares against the Nasdaq-100 index (NDX) benchmark:

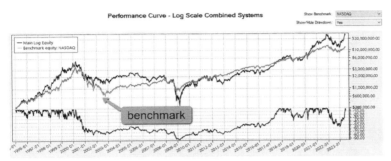

Figure 2.3: Performance of the Nasdaq-100 system as compared to NDX benchmark (gray curve).

The drawdowns, though... That 93% drawdown in 2009, and the duration of the maximum length of the drawdown is enormous – more than 17 years!

Clearly, this would not be a viable system option. Yes, the system makes money, and yes, it even beats the NDX index (NASDAQ 100 index), but it's just way too scary to deal with and rely on in live trading.

Let's Improve This System Further

So, let's use exit rules to improve our system. We should not be holding a stock that is failing so much that it will feel like we will lose it all.

How about if we say:

- We will exit from the stock if it drops below the original entry price by 20%.
- Also, what if we say, let's trail our stop loss behind when the stock does go up. In other words, we will use a Trailing Stop. Let's give it 25%. This means that if the stock rose and then started to drop from its highest price, we will be stopped out when it drops 25% from that highest price.

Let's see what will happen now to the curve and stats:

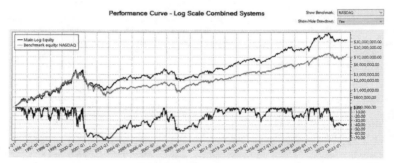

Figure 2.4: Performance of a Nasdaq-100 system with stop loss and trailing stop.

Quick stats:

- CAGR: 17.88%
- Maximum Drawdown: 76.81%
- Maximum Duration of the Drawdown: around 7.5 years

Not bad, right?

Let's compare it to the index:

	S&P 500 B&H*	NDX Index Performance	Nasdaq-100 System With 10 Positions
CAGR	8.27%	13.61%	17.88%
Max Drawdown	56.58%	82.90%	76.81%
Max Duration of the Drawdown	7.2 years	15.6 years	7.5 years

*B&H: Buy and Hold

Table 2.1: Comparison of S&P 500, NDX Index and Nasdaq-100 system with ten positions including exits.

Now, we're clearly outperforming the NDX index, and our biggest drawdown is now about 76%, which is still not at an acceptable level for real live trading. Yet, it clearly beats what we had before.

Still, you can see where by setting more logical rules we can start massaging the results, and it will be much easier to deal with the swings (ups and downs) of the account's equity.

At this point you might be wondering why we chose 20% for the stop loss and 25% for the trailing stop. Why not 30%, or even 5%, as a lot of people think that the smaller the better?

These are all good questions and may lead to a very big topic of how to not overoptimize your rules, which could be a separate full book on its own. I'll just touch on this briefly here.

Overoptimization

Imagine if we now try to run the simulation and seek to find the best stop loss and trailing stop combination that produces the best results. We might find something like that in this example: 23.8% for Stop Loss and 27.64% for the Trailing Stop.

Does it mean that this is truly the best? Could it be just luck this sequence of trades produced the best results, and a different sequence would not repeat these numbers?

The unfortunate part is that most likely the latter could be the case here. This is because if we continue optimizing the parameters, we will eventually find the right combination for the past data. Our optimized parameters would avoid all, or maybe most, of the landmines and thus improve the results. It would just be wishful thinking, though, as once you start going live with your system, it will not produce the same results as you've expected it to do.

This is exactly what happens to a lot of people who like to run the "optimize" button on some popular software packages. Also, this is what I don't recommend doing at all.

When I check with our students on weekly calls as to what they've accomplished, the first thing I ask is if there is some strange number for any parameter that they've used. As an example, if they put 26.4% trailing stop, I immediately know that they have tried to overoptimize this parameter. My leading question always is: why is it 26.4% and not 30% or 25% or even 20%?

What happens to the system if you try 20, 25, 30%?

Do you get similar results in general or different results altogether? How stable are your results? Do they change a lot just because you've slightly changed your parameter, or do they produce similar CAGR, drawdowns, and other statistics? The statistics would not be identical, but they need to be in the same ballpark of what you're expecting.

All these questions lead us to the key idea of how to do it right, which is a little bit of an art when "good enough" is much better than the "best" parameter.

Can We Improve It Further Without Overoptimizing?

Indeed, we can. What would you say is a pattern you see here? Let me give you a hint: when the market is going down, will the system also go down?

I hope you've answered: yes, it looks that way.

So, can we use this knowledge to our advantage? Sure, we can!

We can put a blanket statement to our rules set:

- If the market symbol, in this case, the NDX index (aka Nasdaq-100 Index), is going down, then we should not open any new positions.
- To clarify the rule above, we need to be more precise at what it means to go down: if the NDX index's price is below the index's price moving average of 252 days

(remember, it's one year of trading), then we will not allow opening any new positions.

What will happen then is once we're stopped out either via a stop loss or our trailing stop, and NDX index's price is below its 252 days moving average, then we will just sit in cash.

Yes, you've heard me right. We will sit in cash! Sometimes, sitting in cash is a much better option for you than trying to always be in the market and trade something.

Take a look at the results with this addition:

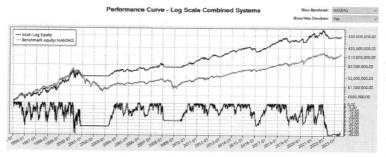

Figure 2.5: Performance of the Nasdaq-100 system with the market entry rule introduced.

Do you see how we're not only outperforming the NDX index now but also have much smaller drawdowns are?

Here are the statistics for this system:

- CAGR: 19.06%
- Maximum Drawdown: 47.41%
- Maximum Duration of the Drawdown: around four years

Really getting better now! Losing half of your equity is still not fun but compared to 70%+ losses or even holding individual stocks with 90%+ losses, it is not even comparable.

	S&P 500 B&H*	NDX Index Performance	Nasdaq-100 System Including Market Entry
CAGR	8.27%	13.61%	19.06%
Max Drawdown	56.58%	82.90%	47.41%
Max Duration of the Drawdown	7.2 years	15.6 years	4 years

*B&H: Buy and Hold

Table 2.2: Comparison of the S&P 500, the NDX Index, and the Nasdaq-100 system with ten positions including Market Entry filter idea.

Also, do you notice how consistent the system becomes over time? It reacts to adverse market conditions in the same way even though we've tested it over a 28-year span.

What if I now say to myself: *Why can't we tighten the trailing stop a little bit? Will it help us?*

Let's find out if we put a 20% trailing stop now instead of the original 25%.

We get the following stats:

- CAGR: 21.80%
- Maximum Drawdown: 45.89%
- Maximum Duration of the Drawdown: around 3.5 years

If we put a 15% trailing stop, then we get the following stats:

- CAGR: 19.31%
- Maximum Drawdown: 53.21%
- Maximum Duration of the Drawdown: around four years

As you can see, it started to help us, but then it degraded the performance when the trailing stop became too tight. This is because stocks have a lot of noise in their price moves – up or down. This noise is there due to all the different participants getting in and out of their positions all the time; so we need to give some space for the stock price to play out and see which way the actual price is pushed.

That's where it becomes a little bit of an art, but you can see the dynamic of what the rules do to the system's performance and choose the most stable parameters. This way, if in the future that noise changes a little bit to be more or less from what it was in the past, then we will still reap the benefits of our system.

In our case, I'll keep the trailing stop at 20% for now in our system, but notice I didn't even test 21%, 22%, etc. I'm trying to find some stable parameters that give me acceptable results within a range of values. In case you already have a question about "a stable system," I'll touch on what it means later in the book. This is called robustness testing, so stay tuned for that part.

	S&P 500 B&H*	NDX Index Performance	Nasdaq-100 System Including Market Entry & 20% Trailing Stop
CAGR	8.27%	13.61%	21.80%
Max Drawdown	56.58%	82.90%	45.89%
Max Duration of the Drawdown	7.2 years	15.6 years	3.5 years

*B&H: Buy and Hold

Table 2.3: Comparison of S&P 500, the NDX Index, and the Nasdaq-10 system with ten positions including Market Entry filter idea and updated Trailing Stop set to 20%.

RULES WILL HELP US:

- Create conditions for when we enter and exit from a stock.
- Minimize risks.
- Increase our returns.
- Eliminate emotions and guesswork.
- Follow proven rules.
- Validate rules through backtesting.
- Avoid over-optimization, as it may not work in live trading.

CHAPTER 3

Introduction To The Approach
And Main Definitions We Will Use

Technical Analysis or Fundamental Approach?

This question comes up all the time for a lot of people. There is a saying, though: there are as many ways to make money in the market as there are traders there.

There is no right or wrong answer to which analysis to use to make money. Warren Buffet is using a **fundamental** (or rather, more accurately, value-based) approach. This means that you are acting as a pseudo-accountant and look at all kinds of public company financials to determine if you want to buy or sell a specific company's stock.

Although this approach works, too, I'm personally not a fan of using it in my testing. There are several reasons for that, which a lot of people may disagree with me, but hear me out and see what we will be using throughout the rest of this book (including the Nasdaq-100 system we've created so far):

- Timing of when to enter and when to exit is much harder to do. You may see the company has great potential and has an undervalued stock price, but it may take years for that upside to realize.
- You can tie up your money with the stocks without the clear objective on when to sell it if it goes up or down.
- You can experience tremendous drawdowns due to the above factors. This is similar to what we've already covered in our buy-and-hold strategy of individual stocks.
- Companies don't report their financials daily and, although it's monitored by the SEC, they can fudge their data to make their reports more appealing to the investors. In other words, historical data for financials is not as reliable as price information of the stock.

These are the main challenging points of using the fundamentals approach all by itself.

Now, let's move on to a second group of purist traders who use **technical analysis**.

These types of traders use all kinds of technical patterns to decide what to do in the market. Some use Chart Patterns; some use just pricing information, such as Open, High, Low, Close prices, and Volume. In some cases, this would be pure price or a derivative of that price, and maybe a combination of price plus volume to get some kind of a value that they can then use in their decision-making.

We will be in the camp of the latter case of traders since our approach is all about trying to create a set of rules that we can automate as much as possible.

What we won't be doing is using chart patterns. We will be trying to systematize our rules, and we will be using indicators for that.

Indicators: What And Why?

What are these price-based and volume-based values then? This is what is called an *indicator*. If you're already familiar with the indicators and what they do, then you can just skip to the next chapter. Keep in mind, though, that we will be using indicators throughout the remainder of this book. As such, make sure that you know all of them, because then it will be so much easier to understand how the systems are built.

Here is a full list of indicators we will be looking at in our systems:

- Price (mostly Closing price of the stock)
- Dollar Volume and Volume
- Rate of Change (ROC)
- Relative Strength Index (RSI)
- Average Directional Index (ADX)
- Average True Range (ATR)
- Percentage of ATR value (ATR%)
- Historical Volatility (HV)
- Simple Moving Average (SMA)
- Exponential Moving Average (EMA)

- Donchian Channel
- Keltner Channel
- Bollinger Bands

As you can see, there are not too many indicators, but these would be enough to create some very interesting results. Some might argue that this is a lot of indicators, but this is only a small fraction of many that exist out there. This is just a drop in the bucket.

Let's go over these in a little more detail. I'm not going to go into a lot of in-depth discussion on each one of them as you can easily find them on the internet too.

Price

This could be self-explanatory, with one little twist: for all our current calculations, we will be using the Daily Closing price as our main price for all the indicators and price filters.

The reason why we will be using the Closing price is that the systems we're talking about here are all based on daily price movements. We're not really concerned about any intraday movements that occur during the day. Also, in most cases, we're not even really concerned about the High, Low, or Open price, other than for backtesting purposes to simulate the correct results for our orders or to discover if our intraday profit targets are hit.

In some cases, for our systems, we also want to make sure that we don't enter into very cheap stocks, also known as *penny stocks.* This is because these stocks live in their own world per se. Institutions don't trade them, and that means that the movements of how they can rise, and fall are mostly affected by retail customers.

On top of that, the slippage of order fills can be really horrendous. This is due to the rounding issues and usually the volume of trading is very low for these types of stocks.

That's the reason why we use Price as a filter to work only with these types of stocks, or to deliberately say we only want to trade stocks where institutional players are playing too.

Price can change all the time, and to make sure we don't accidentally get into a stock that is right on the border of being called a penny stock, we can average out that price over a period of time. That's where you might see a notation in later chapters with systems such as "greater than $1 over 25 days." This means that we're averaging out the price over the last 25 days, and it must be at a minimum of $1 or more. It won't guarantee we will avoid penny stocks altogether, but at least it will lower the probability of that occurrence for sure.

Dollar Volume And Volume

Dollar Volume and Volume are important measurements we use to understand if we have enough liquidity for a given stock. Slippage is already mentioned above, but besides the slippage problem, there are other things that require us to make sure we have enough liquidity.

When we start talking about Shorting stocks, meaning borrowing them and then selling, that also means if there is not enough liquidity for that stock, it's possible there is no shorting available for it.

Our simulation software can't know if shorts were available for the stocks. This is because the data provider we would use will not be tied to your broker account, and shorting is applicable only to what your broker can provide you.

Our main goal, then, is to make sure we don't lie to ourselves with nicely looking curves on the tests. We're trying to ensure our simulation will be as close to the experience as possible to what we will get in live trading. That's why we will use Dollar Volume averaging to make sure we have enough liquidity.

Dollar Volume is called that because it takes your current Closing price of the stock and multiplies it by that same day's volume of how many shares exchanged hands. So, each stock will have a different Dollar Volume but, in most cases, we can approximate it to a minimum threshold that we will use in our systems.

Rate Of Change (ROC)

Actually, we've touched on this one already, and as a reminder, this indicator measures the following:

- How much the price has changed in the given time, also known as "lookback."

Imagine what you're trying to do is to calculate what the return was on the price in X days. For example, if a stock's price grew from $100 to $110 in one year, this means the stock made $10, or $10 divided by the original $100, which makes it 10%. So, our Rate of Change (ROC) is 10%.

We can use the following notation to indicate the lookback we're working with for it: ROC (252) = 10%. This means we are saying that the Rate of Change of 252 days is equal to 10%.

If we want to have a rule that says: I want to work with stocks that have a rate of change greater than 10% in a one-year span, then we can express it as: ROC (252) > 10%.

Does it make sense so far? We will use similar notations later. The main thing to understand here is normally we use some kind of a lookback for an indicator and then a threshold value to work with. This will become a normal occurrence.

Relative Strength Index (RSI)

So far, we have talked about different indicators that help us figure out the volatility or how the price changes over time. There is another set of indicators out there that are used to try to predict if the stock is about to hit the top or the bottom of the price, in other words, if the stock's price is ready to change direction.

These types of indicators are generally called oscillators. They change their values, normally, from 0 to 100 and back. They oscillate.

Sometimes, they are also labeled as *momentum* indicators because they supposedly show if there is a lot of momentum building up in the price movement (either up or down). I personally prefer naming them an oscillator.

You might read in other books people mention that a stock was in an oversold condition or an overbought condition. When you see that definition, it most likely refers to one of these oscillator indicators. If the price went up really fast for the stock, that creates a condition that we can categorize as overbought, meaning there is a very good likelihood the stock was bought so much lately that an inevitable pullback is coming for it.

People who were very excited about the latest rally for the stock will start selling to lock in their profits. This fuels more selling because others, who didn't want to sell, see the price starts to drop, and they want to jump on the same bandwagon to lock in whatever profits they have accumulated there. It's human psychology at play here.

In our tests we will use a commonly used oscillator: Relative Strength Index (RSI).

In the example below, I'm using RSI (7) to see how it can show us the overbought and oversold conditions.

Typically, people use different thresholds for these overbought or oversold conditions: 80 and 20, respectively, in this case. What it means is if the value of an RSI goes above 80, then you can consider this to be an overbought state. If the value of an RSI goes below 20, then we will consider this to be an oversold state.

What people might not realize is that these overbought or oversold conditions are not a guarantee the price is reaching the top or the bottom.

A lot of times RSI can reach a value of 99 and stay there for quite some time, or vice versa, it can reach almost 0 and stay there. This is all a game of odds, and normally you'd need to have some other indicator helping you out to see if it's time to buy or sell a stock along with the RSI indicator.

For example, traders may combine the RSI with trend-following indicators like moving averages to determine the overall direction of the market. If the RSI indicates an overbought condition but the stock is still in a strong uptrend according to moving averages, traders might hold off on selling as the trend suggests the price could continue to rise.

Figure 3.1: RSI (7) is plotted for IBM stock.

Average Directional Index (ADX)

When we know about the volatility of the stock and what price it has and what kind of dollar volume it has, we might want to see how strong the moves are regardless of the direction that the price takes.

Here we can use the ADX for this reason. This particular indicator can show us in absolute terms how strong the stock is over a period of time regardless of whether it goes up or down during that time. This is quite useful to put it against other stocks for side-by-side comparison without the worry that we need to normalize the values based on the price of each stock. The ADX is already normalized.

Take a look at that same IBM stock with the ADX (14):

Figure 3.2: ADX (14) for IBM stock. Notice how the value of the ADX changes regardless of up or down movement of the stock.

Notice how the value of the ADX is changing based on the strength of the price movement and not the direction of the price movement. This is the important thing to understand with ADX because it's a *directionless* indicator.

The indicator itself has other components, which you can plot on the graph, but for our purposes, we will be using just the actual ADX value for our filtering of stocks in our systems.

Average True Range (ATR)

We will use different indicators for different reasons. ATR, and a few others, will be used to *measure volatility of stocks.*

What does volatility of stocks mean? This means how fast the stock is changing price over time. Think of it like a bipolar behavior of the stock's price: the bigger the price swings are, the higher the volatility.

Volatility measurement is very important for us. Some stocks barely change price over time, and some move up and down like crazy. This is where we can decide if we want to work with slow-moving stocks or stocks where the price can change quickly. It all depends on what kind of ideas we have about stocks.

The ATR measures how the price of the stock changes from day to day and within the day itself. In other words, the simplest case is we take the High of the daily price and Low of the daily price and find how big that movement was for that day. Then, we also want to make sure that we take into account any gaps that formed between the previous day's price and today's prices while the market was closed.

All of this is then used to measure the True Range for that day, which is then added to all previous True Ranges, smoothed out for the chosen lookback period. It may sound complicated, but in reality, just think of it as a measurement of how our price can fluctuate over a period of time.

You can easily plot an ATR on the chart on most popular sites, such as Yahoo! Finance or TradingView.com.

Figure 3.3: ATR (14) for IBM stock. Notice how ATR values change as the stock's price changes over time.

Notice how the ATR value changes when the stock's price changes over time. The bigger the price moves, the larger the ATR becomes.

The ATR value is depicted in actual dollars smoothed out for the chosen lookback period. That's why, when you plot cheaper stocks, you'll see smaller ATR values; for more expensive stocks, it will be much larger values.

Percentage Of ATR Value (ATR%)

Once again, the ATR by itself is measured in the actual dollar value. What this means is we really need to be able to compare different stocks side by side.

How would we accomplish that? The solution is easy: divide the absolute value of the ATR by the stock price. This means we are normalizing the values, and it won't matter if the stock is $1 or $1000 - the normalized value will tell us if the volatility of these stocks is the same or not.

That's why we normally use ATR% to filter out stocks by their volatility. And we will use the actual ATR value for things like stop loss value or order value.

Historical Volatility (HV)

Historical Volatility (HV) is another way to measure stock volatility. Its mathematical formula is a little bit more involved, and I'd recommend reading about it in more detail in other sources.

In a nutshell, HV uses standard deviation and mean (average of the price) to figure out how the price can vary over time.

Here is an example of what it looks like for the same IBM stock, next to the ATR (14) (see Figure 3.2):

As you can see, given the same lookback (14 days in the example), we get quite similar results for both ATR and HV but with one big difference: ATR is measured in actual dollar moves of the stock, and HV is measured in the percentage deviation of the stock value.

For this reason, HV is already normalized and can be used directly to compare different stocks side by side, just like what the ATR% does for us.

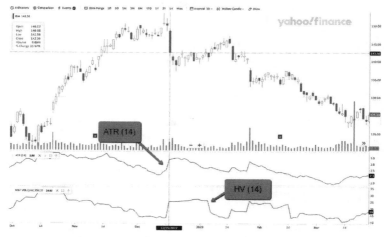

Figure 3.4: HV(14) and ATR(14) for the same IBM stock.

Simple Moving Average (SMA)

Another very common indicator is the Simple Moving Average (SMA). You can find it mentioned in a majority of technical-based systems. It's such an easy indicator that it has become the most commonly used indicator by a lot of people.

The idea behind it is very simple: we take the Closing prices of the chosen lookback period, sum them all up, and then divide them by the lookback. So, if we take SMA (10), that means we will take ten days of the Closing prices, sum them up, and then divide them by ten. The value that we will get is the average price for the past ten days.

The reason why SMA is called Simple Moving Average is that we now have this window of the lookback keep moving in time as we slide it into the future or past.

The smaller the lookback, the faster the SMA. Faster in terms of how it tracks the smoothed-out price behind:

Figure 3.5: SMA (10) and SMA (50) for IBM stock.

Notice how the SMA (10) is tracking the price much closer as compared to the SMA (50). This is because the longer the lookback, the more data points are averaged out.

This leads to the fact that the SMA is always a lagging indicator. It lags behind the actual price. Sometimes it's good for what we're looking for in our systems, and sometimes it's not. It's good when we're trying to smooth things out and get rid of noise. It can be bad because it takes time for the SMA value to catch up, especially on the longer lookbacks.

Exponential Moving Average (EMA)

Since the SMA lags behind, people tried to come up with different ways of ensuring we can still get rid of the noise in the price movements while lagging less.

EMA was invented for this exact scenario: it favors more recent prices, so it lags less than SMA, but it still smooths out prices.

Take a look at the comparison of the identical lookbacks SMA (21) vs EMA (21):

Figure 3.6: SMA (21) vs EMA (21) for IBM stock.

Notice how the blue EMA (21) repeats the price much faster compared to the red SMA (21).

Again, this could be helpful and might not be helpful too. That's why in some cases we might want to experiment with SMA, and in some cases, we will use EMA.

Donchian Channel

This fancy sounding indicator is nothing more than a simple measurement of what the highest or lowest price was in the past X days ago. In other words, what was the highest high in, let's say, the last 100 days, and what was the lowest low in the same 100 days.

Simple, right? If we plot it on the graph, we might get something like this channel, and the reason that it's called a channel is we track both the highest high and lowest low for the X days ago:

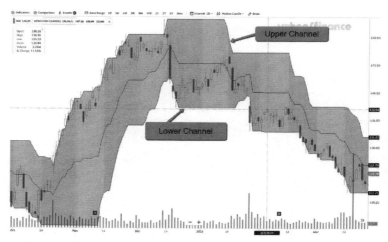

Figure 3.7: Donchian channel (20) plotted on IBM stock.

One more additional piece of information we need to be aware of for the Donchian channel is all of the channel values are constructed based on the Closing Price for each trading day. It means you can see that sometimes the wicks (high or low points of the bars) can exceed the channel values. This is normal and actually helpful for us to issue our signals in the systems.

Keltner Channel

This one also sounds quite fancy, but it's also very simple to understand because you already know about EMA and ATR indicators. This indicator combines the two together to arrive at the channel: EMA is the center line that tracks where this channel is going, and ATR is the width (or height to be more geometrically correct) of that channel:

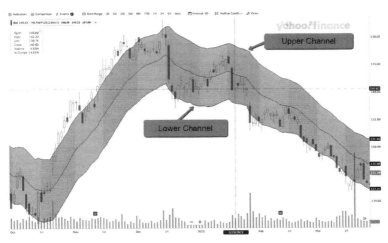

Figure 3.8: Keltner (20, 2) plotted for IBM stock.

In the graph above, we've plotted Keltner (20, 2). The center line is the EMA (20), and the upper and lower channel values are 2 ATR (20) values added or subtracted from the EMA (20) value. In other words, we calculate ATR (20), multiply the resulting value by 2, and then add and subtract that value from the EMA (20) value to plot the upper boundary and the lower boundary, respectively.

The key idea behind using Keltner Channels is to be able to see how the price acts compared to both the smoothed-out general direction (EMA portion) and any volatility of the price (ATR portion).

Bollinger Bands

You might be wondering if this one is different from the other channels because it's called Bollinger Bands, but in all honesty,

I think it should've been called Bollinger Channels. Alas, it predates other channels, and the name stuck, hence it's called Bollinger Bands.

Bollinger Bands are almost the same as Keltner Channel, except the center line used for it is constructed from SMA, and the bands, the actual channels, are made up from the Standard Deviation values for the price of the stock:

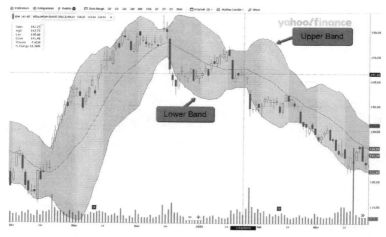

Figure 3.9: Bollinger Bands (20, 2) for IBM stock.

In the above example, we've used Bollinger Bands (20, 2), which means it's SMA (20) for the center line and 2 STDEV (20). STDEV is the notation I'm using for Standard Deviation of the price. It's the same type of Standard Deviation used for Historical Volatility.

The idea behind the Bollinger Bands indicator is the same as for Keltner Channel because there is a smoothing factor (SMA portion) and a volatility of the stock (STDEV portion).

Why Bother With The Indicators In The First Place?

There are so many different indicators out there now. Some of them sound really scary and fancy, some mysterious, some simple, but the sheer amount of them can intimidate a lot of people. On top of this, you can always hear someone claiming their indicator is the holy grail of trading, and you will get a 90%+ win rate by using it.

Let me, hopefully, dispel for you that there is no holy grail in any of the indicators. Pretty much all indicators are working based on some historical information. What it means is the "predictions" these indicators produce are not really predictions but rather an indication of what could possibly happen (that's why they are named as "indicators").

Indicators are useful because it all comes down to statistics. Trading is about gaining a statistical advantage and not really looking at each and every trade as a win-or-die event.

That's why we use indicators to see if we can get that advantage by comparing where our current price is compared to some value produced by the indicator.

In other words, sometimes you can easily replace one indicator for another for the same system and get similar results. Like, I can use Bollinger Bands for a system and then just replace them with Keltner Channel instead. The reason why it would work is these indicators are similar in nature. That's why you can try to group them based on what they do and then just pick whichever one you like for your system's development.

This is where it's useful to pick indicators so you can easily explain to yourself how they work. You might not know all the ins and outs of how it arrives at its value, but you need to know what it's doing.

It's the same as for the actual system's development, where the more you understand what your system does, the better off you are in the long run.

You won't abandon your system and switch to the new one. You won't freak out if your system is going into a drawdown. You won't feel a Fear of Missing Out (FOMO), or too much greed for that matter, too.

And how do you achieve all this? It's done by creating systems with indicators that are easy to understand and to use. Simple systems are always the most robust and easiest to use.

Don't fall into the trap of "my indicator is much more superior than this one." It's better to go with the basic ones than look for something unknown.

The more important part of using indicators is the lookback duration and not which indicator you pick. The 200-day Keltner Channel or Donchian Channel give quite similar results, but a 50-day lookback would make a big difference for the same indicators.

INDICATORS:

- There are a lot of indicators available, but none of them is the holy grail.
- You don't need to use all of them to make money. Pick only the ones you know and understand.
- The simpler the indicator, the better. Keep this motto in mind.
- Indicators can be grouped into similar action groups. Choose the ones that align with creating your trading rules.
- The lookback period for an indicator significantly impacts the end result of your trading systems. The difference is much more pronounced compared to choosing a different indicator of the same kind.

Order Types: What And How To Use

There are several order types that can be used to open positions. Some are exotic, and some are so common that people don't even realize they are using them.

I prefer the approach of "simpler the better," which means we will use four common order types. These will be enough to demonstrate how to use different conditions and ideas together to create our rule-based systems.

- Market On Open
- Market On Close

- Limit Order
- On Stop Order

Market On Open Order Type

This is the most commonly used order type by many traders who trade based on End Of Day (EOD) data. It means submitting an order **before** the market opens each trading day, and as soon as the market opens, this order will be executed.

We will also trade in all our examples based on End Of Day (EOD) data. There is no need to do it more frequently if you don't want to have more complicated software and watch the screen all day. Besides, as you will see, it provides sufficient returns for a nice balance between living your life and the amount of work needed to run your systems. You can spend as little as five-to-ten minutes a day operationally running these systems and do whatever else you desire.

With this out of the way, let's talk in more detail about the Market On Open order type.

Market On Open consists of a Market order, which is scheduled to be active as soon as the market opening bell rings. If you already know what a Market Order is and how it operates, then it's quite simple to understand what a Market On Open order does.

Just to make sure we're on the same page, let me briefly go through an overview of what a Market Order is and how it works under the hood:

- It's an order type where we ask our broker to buy (if we pick Long positions) shares of the stock at the currently available price.

- The currently available price is based on what market makers and other participants in the market set their Bids and Asks. Bids are when they say they don't want to pay more than the Bid Price to buy your stock and Asks are when they say they don't want to sell you a stock for less than the Ask price. Therefore, the Bid price is always smaller than the Ask price.

- There is always a gap between Bid and Ask for each stock. This is called Level I Bid/Ask or bid/ask spread or simply price spread.

- There are a lot of participants with their own ideas on what type of Ask or Bid to set. This leads to a lot of open orders sitting there, waiting for customers to sweep them up. If you can see these levels, it's called Level II Bid/Ask Order Book. You will see a lot of Bids and a lot of Asks as they form layers of different price points for the stock.

- When a participant comes in and says they want to use a Market Order, it means their broker will start sweeping through all the Level II orders to fill their request. If they've asked to Buy X number of shares, then their broker will go to all the Asks and start filling their order until they have their shares. If they've asked their broker to Sell X number of shares, then their broker will sweep through all the Bids to fill their orders. Sweeping means the broker will go from Level II resting orders one by one until the market order is filled. For example, if they requested to buy 1000 shares but the closest Ask has only 100 shares, the next Ask has another 200 shares, and the next one has 2000 shares, their broker will sweep through these Asks to fill the 1000 shares order by taking all of the first Ask shares, second Ask shares, and some of the third Ask shares.

- This can lead to *Slippage* on the order, where they'll be filled at the averaged-out price of all the Ask orders from the Level II order book that were swept by their market order.

- This way, Market Orders always take liquidity from the market since they're sweeping all the outstanding Asks and Bids (depending on whether it's a Buy or Sell market order).

As you can see, a Market Order is quite a simple order type. That's why using Market On Open is simple too. One side effect of using a Market On Open order specifically is since all of these End of Day traders use a lot of them, all of these orders have to be executed almost at the same time – as soon as the *opening bell* rings.

This possibly leads to a fast sweeping of Level II Order Book entries and results in quite some slippage on your orders. So, keep in mind that for us, we will be using some slippage assumptions to fully simulate what would happen during this Market On Open time when we are getting filled.

Normally, this order type will be used to get into positions, but in some cases, we can use it to close them out too. It all depends on what kind of ideas we have for our systems.

The benefit of using a Market Order is you're almost guaranteed the order execution (as long as there are resting Level II orders). This can be an important ingredient for your system if you want to be in a stock no matter what, although you're forfeiting the best fill price though, which in some cases is acceptable.

Market On Close Order Type

This is also a Market Order, but it's used now at the end of the trading day and will become active as soon as the market *closing bell* rings.

This order also causes a big sweep of the Level II Order Book, but unlike Market On Open, typically there are a very large number of participants, and slippage is much smaller than what Market On Open can incur.

Normally, we can use this order type to close out our positions, but in some cases, we can still use this order type as our opening position order too. It all depends on what types of rules we're trying to use for our systems and what kind of ideas we have.

Limit Order Type

Now, remember all these participants with Bids and Asks and Level II Order Book? A lot of these orders are Limit orders.

These orders are sitting in the market and waiting for a Market Order to sweep them up. They are bringing liquidity into the market, and without them, there would probably be no market to work with.

With a limit order, we are firmly standing our ground in the request and saying that we won't allow our broker to buy the stock unless the price on the market falls below our Limit Order.

What does it mean to "fall below it" then? It's when your limit order becomes the highest Bid in this case before the smallest Ask. So, when a market order comes in and wants to sweep your bid, your order will be executed.

In other words, if we use a Limit order, we need to be aware of a few things:

- If the market moves away from it (current highest Bid for a Long Limit order), then we won't be executing anytime soon, unless the market price comes back down to us.
- There is no slippage with a Limit order in the absolute terms. Unlike a market order, there is nothing to sweep in this case, and we will be either executed or not.
- We might be executed partially though if the market order, which came in to sweep us, didn't need as many shares as we had in our Limit order. For example, we've set a 1000 shares Limit Order, but some market order came in and got only 200 shares out of that. So, we will still have our Limit order but now sitting at 800 shares, which would be waiting for another market order to sweep our shares from us.
- If we've submitted our Limit order (for the Long system it will be a Bid) before the market opens but it's already exceeding the current lowest Ask (the price of our Limit order requested is higher than the lowest Ask), then our

Limit order will be executed as if it's a Market On Open order once the market opens up.

- If our Limit Order was executed as if it's a Market Order, then we will incur slippage similar to what a market order does.

Key things to remember about Limit order type that are worth repeating: the Limit order might not get executed on a trading day if the market walks away from it, and it could be executed as a Market On Open order if the market already gapped down or up depending on the Limit Order type (sell or buy).

We will use Limit Order types extensively for our systems when we want to explore the above features, where we want to be selective at what price we want to get into a position.

On Stop Order Type

This order type is a combination of a couple of things:

- An order is put in the market, but what sits there is a trigger, waiting for the market to come to us.
- Once that trigger is executed, then the order activates as a Market Order and will work as a regular market order.

This order type is normally used for breakouts. When we want to make sure that the price has to go up high enough before we will get into a position (for the Long position).

Make sure you understand, though, that the On Stop Order is essentially a delayed (by the trigger) Market Order. During the day, the slippage for a Market Order is the highest due to the smaller number of participants and wider Level II Order Book, which will lead to a much larger slippage and the worst fill price for your positions.

ORDER TYPES:

- We will use very simple order types for our systems.
- **Market On Open**: It's a market order activated at the *opening bell* for the market.
- **Market On Close**: It's a market order activated at the *closing bell* for the market.
- **Limit Order**: It's an order we want the market to come to us before we allow a position to be opened. For a Long position, we will wait for the market to come *down* to us. For a Short position, we will wait for the market to come *up* to us.
- **On Stop Order**: It's a market order but with a trigger when it can be activated. We will wait for the market to come to us to activate that trigger and then execute our market order. For a Long position, we will wait for the market to come *up* to us. For a Short position, we will wait for the market to come *down* to us. This is basically the opposite of what the Limit order does.
- Slippage is highest for Market Orders when executed during the day. On Stop Order will have the highest slippage.
- Limit Order and On Stop Order might not get executed at all during the day if the market walked away from them.
- Limit Order might be executed partially.

CHAPTER 4

A Suite Of Systems Is Even Better Than Just Rules!

What Is A Suite Of Systems?

So far, we've created our first Nasdaq-100 system above. It doesn't mean that this is what we will trade by itself. In theory, yes, we can trade this system. It's better than any buy-and-hold versions we had, especially if you consider the drawdowns. So why not just trade this system?

I have a gazillion reasons why that should not be the case, but will you just take my word for it?

I think I need to run through a few examples to make my point.

Before I do that, I need to at least explain what a Suite of System is because I'll be using this concept going forward.

It's quite simple, though: it's just *a set of systems put together.*

The question is: which systems?

That's right, that's the key. We don't want to just have more of the same systems because otherwise, all we're doing is getting into the same stocks with the same ups and downs of their prices.

We're looking for systems that get into different stocks, and preferably these stocks are not even correlated in their price movements.

This is what is called a set of **non-correlated systems**.

Another significant side effect of having a lot of systems working at the same time is each individual stock's position in your suite becomes smaller and smaller. It will happen to the point where even if a stock is going down to $0 (company went bankrupt), then it won't be affecting you as much as if you had only one system, and all of your equity was distributed among just ten stocks.

We can see this in action if we build another system. Let's see what will happen next.

The S&P 500 System In Action

What would happen if now we took the same exact rules that we've built above for the Nasdaq-100 system and then reused the parameters with the S&P 500 stock universe instead?

By the way, as a side note, this is how you can also test how robust your system parameters are. If they work on a different set of stocks, then most likely you have reasonably robust and stable system rules. More about robustness testing is discussed later in the book.

I want to iterate here once again that we are going to be using more and more of an "idea-first" approach to layer our ideas and translate them into rules. It's all about understanding what the system is supposed to do and how it should be working.

The idea of using another stock universe is simple. We want to get into stock positions by diversifying our portfolio.

What would be the easiest way to do that? The answer could be simple or could be quite complex.

We can start with a simple solution: we will use another stock universe, meaning that we will have different stocks that we can use for our system. There could be some overlap, but it's not as big as just using the same stock universe.

Since we're venturing into other stock universes, we would need to consider what stocks are a part of them. Some stock universes have a lot of very slow-moving stocks – stocks that don't have liquidity. We would need to deal with that using our rule-based approach to filter them out.

Since the S&P 500 stock universe has stocks that are also cheap, we need to narrow them down to be at least $1 per stock price or above. We need to do it to avoid the realm of penny stocks. Penny stocks live in their own world, and at this point, we don't want to venture there.

And as we've already mentioned, some S&P 500 stocks barely move each day. We're trying to avoid stocks that don't trade much volume, so we don't incur a big slippage on the execution price.

Also, we really don't want to be the biggest participant of the day to buy shares and move the price. Let's avoid any stock that hasn't traded less than 100,000 shares in a day in the last 25 days on average.

Here are all the rules for the same system we had before with the new additions:

- S&P 500 stock universe with all the joiners and leavers from 1995
- We only trade stocks that have been consistently above $1 or more over the last 25 days.
- We only trade stocks that have averaged 100,000 shares per day over the last 25 days.
- We will enter only into ten positions, giving them equal allocation.
- We have a market filter, the NDX Index, so we don't open any new positions if the NDX Index price is below the 252 moving day average price.
- We rank all our stocks by the Highest Rate of Change over the 252 days.
- We enter into a position as a Market On Open order if all of the above rules give us a positive signal.
- We exit if we hit a 20% stop loss.
- We exit if we hit a 20% trailing stop.

This is what we will get:

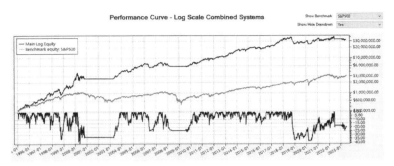

Figure 4.1: Performance of the S&P 500 system. Note that we've used the S&P 500 index as a benchmark there now (red curve).

Here are the statistics for this system:

- CAGR: 17.70%
- Maximum Drawdown: 41.38%
- Maximum Duration of the Drawdown: around 3.7 years

	S&P 500 B&H*	NDX Index Performance	Nasdaq-100 System Including Market Entry & 20% Trailing Stop	S&P 500 System
CAGR	8.27%	13.61%	21.80%	17.70%
Max Drawdown	56.58%	82.90%	45.89%	41.38%
Max Duration of the Drawdown	7.2 years	15.6 years	3.5 years	3.7 years

*B&H: Buy and Hold

Table 4.1: Comparison of the S&P 500 buy-and-hold, the NDX index, the Nasdaq-100 system, and the SP500 system.

It's not a bad system and produces quite nice results. The most notable statistic is that the drawdowns are much smaller than what the Nasdaq-100 system had, yet it's still over 41%.

What will happen if we combine these two systems together? Let's take our full equity, split it up into parts, and give 50% to the Nasdaq-100 system and 50% to the S&P 500 system. This way, we will now be entering into up to 20 positions at any given moment and possibly not even into the same stocks.

In order to make sure that we don't enter into the same positions at any given moment, we will use a trick where we will check which stocks systems we are trying to get before we create our orders. If we already have a position for a stock XYZ in System 1, or we have a candidate for this stock XYZ for both systems, then we will not allow opening two positions and rather choose the next in line stock ABC for System 2.

In this case, we have Nasdaq-100 as our System 1 and S&P 500 as our System 2.

Here are the results:

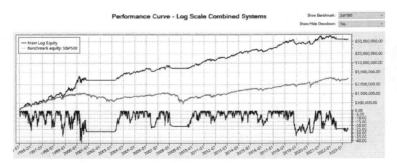

Figure 4.2: Performance of a combined suite of the Nasdaq-100 and the SP500 systems. The S&P 500 index is used as a benchmark curve.

Here are the statistics for this system:

- CAGR: 20.05%
- Maximum Drawdown: 41.87%
- Maximum Duration of the Drawdown: around 3.5 years

	S&P 500 B&H*	NDX Index Performance	Nasdaq-100 System Including Market Entry & 20% Trailing Stop	S&P 500 System	Suite Combo: Nasdaq-100 + S&P 500 Systems
CAGR	8.27%	13.61%	21.80%	17.70%	20.05%
Max Drawdown	56.58%	82.90%	45.89%	41.38%	41.87%
Max Duration of the Drawdown	7.2 years	15.6 years	3.5 years	3.7 years	3.5 years

*B&H: Buy and Hold

Table 4.2: Comparison of the S&P 500 buy-and-hold, the NDX index, the Nasdaq-100 system, the SP500 system, and the Nasdaq-100 + SP500 Suite Combo.

Notice how the resulting curve now produces much better-looking drawdowns. Compare it to Figure 2.5 and Figure 4.1.

We haven't used any leverage, and we have reduced per-stock effective allocation. Meaning that we're now giving each position a much smaller slice of equity. This way, if a stock goes bankrupt, then the effect of this slice would be smaller than when it was a single system.

The drawdowns in this combo are closer to what the S&P 500 system produced, but the CAGR is closer to what the Nasdaq-100 system produced. Which is very nice indeed!

This is how we can start working our way of reducing drawdowns while keeping the same returns or even making them better than before. The suite of systems is working as anticipated and exactly what we're looking for.

Another Set Of Different Systems To Use For Combination Of Systems

The possibilities of what to do from here are pretty much almost endless. We can create systems that will work off specific sectors, or we can use other stock universes that are common, such as the Russell 2000 index set of stocks, or the Russell 3000 index.

Again, the reason why I'm choosing different stock universes is we're trying to avoid getting into the same stocks across multiple systems. We're trying to diversify as much as possible while automatically minimizing each position's size and effect on the overall suite.

Let's come up with another system as our base. We're trying to avoid collisions with the stocks of our Nasdaq-100 and S&P 500 systems, so we might as well try to play it from industry sectors.

When you choose stocks from each sector, you're guaranteed not to see the same stocks from a different sector.

Let's use the *Healthcare Sector* as the stock universe for the next new base system.

The Healthcare Sector has quite a few stocks in it, but that's not the main reason why I've picked it here. Healthcare stocks are notorious for moving a lot in price when some events happen to them.

Remember our main premise is to try to find big winners so we are outperforming the index.

I could've picked the Russell 2000 (which is an index of mid-small cap stocks), or some other stock universe with similar characteristics, but for this exercise, let's start with the Healthcare Sector to see how things can work out.

We will introduce two more things to consider for the system though. This is needed so we can be pickier about which stocks we want to enter into a position. Since we're looking for big movers, we need to consider the volatility of stocks and their price more closely.

Rules for the system:

- Stock universe: any stock that is marked as the Healthcare Sector
- We only trade stocks that have averaged between $1 and $5 over the last 25 days. *We're trying to trade cheaper stocks here, so we allow them to grow fast.*
- We only trade stocks that have averaged 100,000 shares per day over the last 25 days.
- We only trade stocks that have Historical Volatility (HV) values between 40-100 over the last 100 days. *This rule is important to introduce because we want stocks that are moving a lot and not some duds.*
- We will trade a stock only if it's trending higher by making sure that the price of that stock is above an Exponential Moving Average (EMA) of 100 days and 2 ATR values. *You may recognize this as Keltner (100, 2).*

ATR is a measurement of a stock's volatility. In this case we will use 21 days ATR as our value for all ATR calculations.

- We will enter only into ten positions giving them equal allocation.

- We have a market filter NDX Index, so we don't open any new positions if the NDX Index price is below 200 days Simple Moving Average (SMA) price.

- We rank all our stocks by the Highest Rate of Change over the 252 days.

- We enter into a position as an On Stop Order at 2% higher than the previous day's Close price only if all of the above rules give us a positive signal. *This sounds a little more complicated, but what we're looking for here is that the stocks will be going higher the next day before we will allow us to enter into a position. That's why we've picked the On Stop Order type to make sure we will only enter into rallying stocks. This will also give us an additional variety of which stocks we can enter.*

- We exit if we hit a 10% stop loss. *Due to the fact that we use the On Stop Order, we can allow an even tighter stop loss than for the Nasdaq-100 or the S&P 500 system that we've created so far.*

- We exit if we hit a 20% trailing stop.

- We will also exit from all positions if our market filter price goes below the 250-day Simple Moving Average and 2 ATR values. *This is our blanket exit statement in case the market turns south. We will exit all open positions whether they are profitable or losing at the time. We don't care about that. We rely on the fact that the stocks are typically very correlated to the market, so we don't want to incur extra losses in our stocks.*

This sounds complex, but it's easier than you think. We have a very good explanation of what to expect this system can do, so it adheres to all our objectives and ideas.

Why I've picked all these rules?

Here is my rationale:

- I need to define my stock universe and then filter out what I don't want to work with. So, I use a price filter from my idea of working only with cheaper stocks, which I anticipate will rally a lot. It's always much easier for a stock to double its price from $1 to $2 than $1000 stock to go to $2000 value.
- I also filter out and narrow down my stock universe by volatility, and I've picked one of the volatility indicators that we've discussed before: Historical Volatility (HV). HV is a good indicator of how the stock is moving around on a longer-term basis, so we've used 100 days as our measuring lookback. Again, according to our idea, we need stocks not only on a cheaper scale but also these stocks are needed to be known to move a lot. Otherwise, how else do we expect these stocks to grow and multiply their price?
- I personally like breakout moves. That means I'm looking for stocks that should be exceeding some price level first before we want to buy them. In this case, I've used an On Stop Order type, which is accomplishing this idea: we won't buy the stock unless during the day it rises at least 2% (according to our rules) from the previous day's closing price.

- When you go for breakout moves, it also means you're assuming this stock has some kick to that move, aka momentum. This can lead us to the idea that we, to some extent, can tighten the Stop Loss. If we guessed wrong, we would get out fast, but if we guessed right, then we will ride up this momentum by trailing it behind with our Trailing Stop.

Here are the results:

Figure 4.3: Performance of the Healthcare Sector stock universe.

Here are the statistics for this system:

- CAGR: 23.59%
- Maximum Drawdown: 58.78%
- Maximum Duration of the Drawdown: around 3.3 years

Notice how it's behaving differently from the NDX Index benchmark, and that's exactly what we're looking for. This will help us to combine into a suite of systems where they will start helping each other. That's why we don't mind the drawdown in the 1996–1999 timeframe because we know that the SP500 and the Nasdaq-100 systems were working during that time – they will help our suite to have a boost during that time.

At this point, we want to continue expanding our systems for the suite. We want to get more and more systems in the suite to smooth out all these nasty drawdowns for each individual system and at the same time try to keep the high CAGR that we had before.

Let's move on to a different stock universe. This time we will use the same system parameters but using the **_Industrials Sector_** stocks. All we will do is substitute the stock universe from one set to another, leaving all the rules the same as for the Healthcare Sector system:

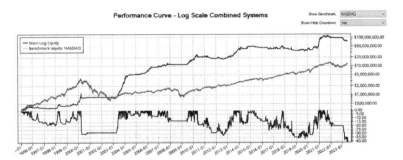

Figure 4.4: Performance of the Industrials Sector stock universe.

Here are the statistics for this system:

- CAGR: 21.59%
- Maximum Drawdown: 41.03%
- Maximum Duration of the Drawdown: around 3.3 years

Again, a quite different curve from the Nasdaq-100 or the SP500 systems, and the Healthcare Sector too. I like the crazy times when it rallies almost vertically up. This will help us a lot with the suite of systems.

How about now we will try the *Energy Sector*. This sector doesn't have as many stocks, so we would need not to limit our price using the maximum price. In order to have more candidates, we have to relax our filter's section of the system a little bit. Plus, quite a few Energy Sector stocks are not as cheap as Healthcare Sector stocks. This ultimately will lead to a less performing system as compared to the Healthcare Sector, but that's not what we're shooting for in this case. Our main objective at the moment is to get a variety of systems where they are not as correlated in their movements.

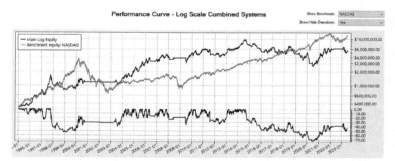

Figure 4.5: Performance of the Energy Sector stock universe.

Here are the statistics for this system:

- CAGR: 10.49%
- Maximum Drawdown: 73.98%
- Maximum Duration of the Drawdown: around 8.8 years

Well, this system doesn't look all that great compared to the other systems, but it still has its place as energy stocks tend to rally when other stocks don't. It's still a positive expectancy system, so we will keep it on our list.

The fact that it's having a very big drawdown is not really a concern once we put things together. That's the biggest takeaway that should be for you: ***Individual system's performances are less important, and what's important is how they all blend together as a suite of systems!***

Now, let's create the ***Financials Sector***. We will use the same approach and the same system as for the Energy Sector.

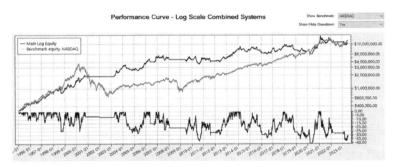

Figure 4.6: Performance of the Financials Sector stock universe.

Here are the statistics for this system:

- CAGR: 13.08%
- Maximum Drawdown: 40.75%
- Maximum Duration of the Drawdown: around 6.2 years

It's different again, and we will keep it too: same deal, same approach. Let's see how it all combines together.

Let's Combine Them Into A Suite Of Systems: Six Systems Together

At this point, let's check what will happen if we combine ALL of these systems together:

- Nasdaq-100 system
- SP500 system
- Healthcare Sector system
- Industrials Sector system
- Energy Sector system
- Financials Sector system

We will allocate 16.66% of our total equity to each system so that it adds up to 100% (the last system in the list will get 16.67%).

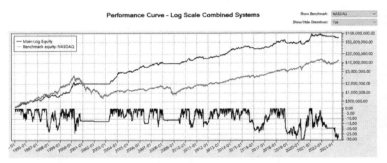

Figure 4.7: Performance of a Suite of Systems: six systems.

Here are the statistics for this Suite of Systems (six systems):

- CAGR: 20.94%
- Maximum Drawdown: 31.10%
- Maximum Duration of the Drawdown: around 3.2 years

What do we see now? How about the drawdowns and the returns? Now, check back to our original Nasdaq-100 system and the SP500 system and other individual systems. Do you see what I mean about how it's more important when and what we combine together? This is the beauty of the Suite of Systems approach!

	S&P 500 B&H*	NDX Index Performance	6-Systems Combo
CAGR	8.27%	13.61%	20.94%
Max Drawdown	56.58%	82.90%	31.10%
Max Duration of the Drawdown	7.2 years	15.6 years	3.2 years

*B&H: Buy and Hold

Table 4.3: Comparison of the S&P 500 buy-and-hold, the NDX index, the six-systems Suite Combo.

Yes, some years we don't outperform the NDX index, but we surely beat it over the long haul, and we definitely don't have to suffer through huge drawdowns. We can smooth them out, and as a net benefit, we will also have smaller and smaller slices for each individual stock that we have a position in. We're, in essence, protecting ourselves not only by diversifying our portfolio but also minimizing risks if something goes wrong on an individual stock's basis.

Adding More Systems To The Mix

I can continue with more and more systems like this. And just to give you an idea, let me add one more system:

We will use the *Information Technology Sector*. It's the same exact system as before for other sectors but just substituting our stock universe:

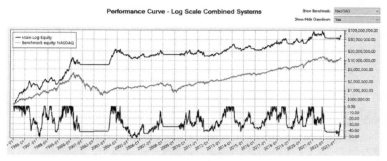

Figure 4.8: Performance of the Information Technology Sector.

Here are the statistics for this system:

- CAGR: 20.82%
- Maximum Drawdown: 53.56%
- Maximum Duration of the Drawdown: around 9.3 years

That rally back in 1995–2000 years is really big! The Dot Com Boom era! It doesn't look like this sector has experienced anything like that ever since, but who is to say that it won't do that again sometime in the future. We want to be ready for such moves, so we will be including this sector in our suite too.

Combined Suite Of Systems: Seven Systems

And now let's combine it all together, giving 14.28% to each system in the mix (and last system a little bit more to round it up to 100% total).

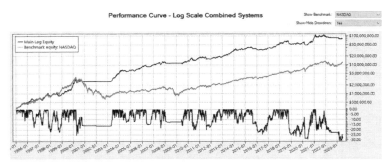

Figure 4.9: Performance of the Suite of Systems: seven systems.

Here are the statistics for this Suite of Systems (seven systems):

- CAGR: 21.52%
- Maximum Drawdown: 29.98%
- Maximum Duration of the Drawdown: around 3.2 years

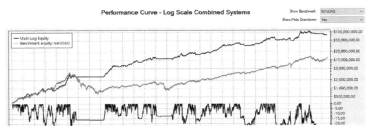

Table 4.4: Comparison of the S&P 500 buy-and-hold, the NDX index, the six-systems Suite Combo, and the seven-systems Suite Combo.

This is getting better and better with each new system I'm adding.

Each individual system by itself is not that impressive due to quite a high level of drawdowns, but once you start combining them together – you get this magic effect of non-correlated systems. Combined together into a suite of systems, we get the results we're looking for!

Isn't it good to see the results materializing as you work on your suite of systems? Do you see what I mean about my Eureka moment that hit me back in 2019, when I decided to give it a try going through *The 30-Minute Stock Trader* book by Laurens Bensdorp?

This is so powerful that it's incredible how even using just Long Only systems, we can minimize our risks and maximize our returns. Compare it to what we had with our Buy-and-Hold approach. It's not even in the ballpark of the performance.

Granted, we can do buy-and-hold of different indexes and even individual stocks and put them together the same way as we did a suite of systems, but without the exit and entry rules, your drawdowns will be several times bigger and much more painful.

We need rules to allow us to make sane actions.

SUITE OF SYSTEMS:

- Each individual system's performance is less important, and we care more about how they combine together.
- Using the Suite of Systems approach allows us to achieve a large CAGR while minimizing drawdowns.
- Not only do we minimize drawdowns, but we also reduce the risks associated with each individual position. Each stock's allocation becomes smaller as we add more systems to our suite.
- The key to combining systems effectively is to avoid getting into the same stock at the same time across multiple systems.

CHAPTER 5

Do You Want To See Even Crazier Returns?

What Else Can Be Done To Have More Non-correlations?

So far in our journey, we've been working with Long Only systems. This is quite normal and considered a safe, traditional route to take. However, the not-so-nice part is that the market, in general, is Long Biased. What this means is the market tends to go up over time, especially in the long run.

Non-correlation would, then, mean trying to find as many instruments as possible that don't move in the same direction at the same time.

We have achieved it to some extent in our Suite of Systems so far, but all these sub-systems have the same long bias correlation: when the market goes up, so will most of the stocks; when the market goes down, so will most of the stocks.

What would allow us to have an extreme non-correlation to long-biased systems?

The answer might be catching a lot of people off guard. How about we talk about Short systems?

Shorting the stock means you sell it when it's high and then buy back when it's low. So, instead of the typical "buy low and sell high" in the Long-Biased world, we will be doing the opposite. Therefore, it should produce an opposite correlation to long-only systems.

We sell high and buy low, getting the difference as our profit. The danger of shorting the stock, though, is if you sold it high, but it continues to rally even higher, you will incur a loss, and that loss can be significantly bigger than even your original investment.

A good example are the meme stocks of 2021 such as GameStop (GME), or AMC (AMC), Bed Bath & Beyond (BBBY, now bankrupt by the way). These stocks were rallying 300% in a day, so you could've seen losses of at least 300% on each position easily. As the saying goes, "the sky is the limit," so shorting is not for everyone.

You really need to test yourself on how you would feel when things like this happen. It's one thing to say, "Sure, no problem, I can handle it," and another thing is actually living through the pain of these types of positions. So, it's always better to try things out in the paper trading account first to see how you can handle it.

Not all short systems are alike though. We would need to review some of the types and see if something can resonate with you.

Different Types Of Short System

There are several types of short systems we can exploit:

- Contrarian short systems
- Go with the trend short systems
- Hedge protection short systems

Contrarian systems are the systems that we can use to go against the main trend. For example, when a stock is rallying hard, the contrarian approach would be trying to short it when it reaches the top of the move.

Go-With-The-Trend short systems are the systems where we'll be shorting stocks that are in a downtrend already. So, the idea behind this approach is to find stocks, which are down trending and have a weak rally. This rally is typically a false rally and can lead to a very nice shorting opportunity.

Hedge protection short systems are the systems that are designed to catch the falling market to protect our long positions. Since we know the majority of long positions will go down with the market, we then can come up with systems to create the protection for our long positions.

For our book, let's just use an example of a Contrarian Short System to prove the point of the non-correlation systems.

You will be amazed at the results so much that I'm sure you'll want to learn more about all other system types. This is normal, don't worry; I've got you covered all the way, just not right now in this book.

Creating a Contrarian Short System

To see extreme non-correlation at play, we will go with the Contrarian Short system.

Other systems are also good, but typically they don't produce high compounded returns, so the effect is less visible. Additionally, they have a different place where they are supposed to work compared to the contrarian system, which can work in pretty much all market conditions. It's a generic short system and it will work well for our suite of systems.

Let's create an idea-first approach for this short system.

Idea: If you observe all the stocks, you will notice that when they go up fast, some people like their profits so much that they start taking them off. When that happens, the price of the stock starts to decline, and it forms what is sometimes called a *pullback*. The price is pulling back from its highest point, that's why the name pullback is commonly used.

You might have also heard it referred to as a "correction." It's the same thing, just a different name. The funny thing is people always try to find some cool names for things they either don't like or don't understand much. By assigning it a term, it becomes a legitimate thing that is not so bad after all. Like, "Oh, this stock has a correction. Don't worry too much. It's temporary and the rise of the stock resumes shortly." Just because you gave it a nice name, it won't make the stock rise when you want it to. That's not how it works. So, we will use the pullback in all of our discussions but understand that it's nothing else but a price change in direction from where it was.

We can consider a Pullback when the price could be pulling up too much from the general direction for the Short system, but for the Long system, a pullback is when the price is pulling down from the general direction of the stock. Keep that in mind.

Let's continue with our short contrarian system, though. The pullback here is when the price has rallied too fast up and is about to pull down.

Even though the stock is making new highs, a lot of times it's primed to pullback at that time. This is where the contrarian idea comes into play of trying to short a stock when it's at its top.

Some people are really ticked off by this approach. It feels like you're going against the flow, and if you were trying to do it manually on a discretionary basis, then it will feel like you're really swimming upstream.

Having it backtested and then traded in an automated fashion does help a lot. Especially since we're looking for short-term moves of catching these small pullbacks when people take their profits.

Why does it work in all kinds of market conditions?

That's because it's human psychology at play. When the stock goes up too fast, then there are a lot of happy people who made money, and they want to make sure they get them as actual profits versus unrealized profits. Once enough of them start taking profits, the stock starts to tip over and triggers even more people into taking profits "while it lasts." This makes the price go down even faster.

At some point, enough people took all their profits and other people who were sitting on the sideline become ready to buy this stock again, and the price of the stock starts to go up again. This is what some people say that you can buy a stock at a *discount*. I personally really don't like that term because we're not in a store where some things are on a discount. It's the market but not the same kind of market. Nobody gives you any discounts here, and the customer is never right in this world of trading.

But I digress, let's come back to our short system.

What we're trying to do is to catch that tipping point and then get out of the stock before buyers will start buying it again.

Obviously, this means it's a short-term move, and that timing is quite crucial.

All of this allows us to start crafting our system rules.

Here are the rules for the system. It may look complex, but again, it's not as complex as you might think.

Most parts are logical components of trying to translate that idea above into the actual rules below:

- Stock universe: All US stock universe. *These are all active stocks that we can find, which were at least more than $1 in price since 1993 and had a volume of at least 100,000 shares* *at some point in time since 1993. This stock universe is not something you can find in sectors or of any known indexes. I've created this stock universe by scanning all of the available stocks using my preferred data provider Norgate (more about my preferred tools and providers at the end of the book).*

- Minimum price is $10. *We're trying to trade stocks where institutions are participating. This is because a) this stock is most likely shortable; b) when institutions take off their profits, they move the price of the stock a lot due to the size of their transactions. Normally institutions participate in stocks that are over $10. This is not a hard rule but more of a rule of thumb.*

- Minimum Dollar Volume of $500,000/day over the average of 20 days

- ATR% (which is a change of Average True Range in percentage) for each stock is more than 5% over an average of ten days. *This way we will get into stocks that are not too slow moving. ATR% is a good measurement of the volatility of stocks. It's more reliable for short-term moves versus Historical Volatility, which is more reliable for long-term moves.*

- We will also measure the strength of the stock by using the ADX indicator. *It allows us to see if the stock was moving either up or down in the short term. Again, we need to get into stocks that move, otherwise the short-term move won't materialize into any significant profits. Our current rule would be: ADX over an average of seven days should be greater than 50. This is quite a strong moving stock.*

- Now, here is the trick to trying to pick the tops:

  - We are looking for an RSI of three days to be over 85 in value. *This tells us if the stock is in an overbought condition in the short-term duration (three days in this case). RSI values go from 0 to 100, where 100 means it's in a completely overbought condition.*
  - AND we want to make sure this stock was up at least two days in a row.
  - *Both of these rules will help us identify if we are possibly hitting the short-term top for this stock, right when people will start taking their profits.*

- Ranking: Once we have all the candidates satisfying the conditions above, we will sort them by the highest RSI of three days.
- So, if all of the above conditions are positive, then we will enter tomorrow as a Limit order equal to the previous day's closing price.
- We will enter into only ten positions at a time and use risk-based allocation, where we measure the risk and buy only enough shares to not exceed the projected loss. *This is called Percent Risk position sizing.*
- We will measure our risk with 2.5 ATR Stop Loss.
- We will exit from the stock if we are either stopped out or we're holding it for over one day. *This is called a Timed Exit. We exit by a specific number of days because we say to ourselves that if a position doesn't work, then we should not be holding it any longer.*
- The exit is a Market On Close order type. *This means we will hold this stock till the market is going to be closed for the*

> *day after our either Stop Loss is triggered, or we've reached our Timed Exit.*

Again, this sounds pretty complicated but if you decipher the moving parts of it, you will see it ends up being in this model:

- Stock Universe
- Entry filters to narrow down the stock universe further by price, dollar volume, or volatility
- Pullback measurements (RSI and consecutive up days in this case)
- Strength measurements (ADX)
- Order entry (Limit order as an additional intraday pullback measurement)
- Stop Loss for an exit
- OR Timed Exit

Using this model, we can craft different short systems.

Let's see what this particular system produces for us:

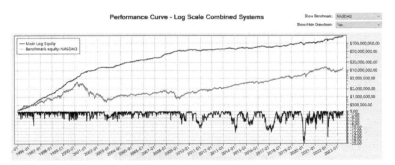

Figure 5.1: Performance of the short contrarian system from 1995 till June 2023.

And the statistics for this system are:

- CAGR: 25.85%
- Maximum Drawdown: 25.97%
- Maximum Duration of the Drawdown: around 2.3 years

This system has a lot of trades because we only hold each stock no longer than one day.

Doesn't it look so much different from what you saw before with our Long systems so far? This is because it's a Short Contrarian system.

This will help us a lot when we combine it with our suite of Long systems because it's clearly non-correlated to the long systems' moves.

Let's See The Magic Of Non-correlated Systems

How about we finally combine it with the rest of our long systems we've compiled so far. Sounds good? I'm sure you're looking at the graph below already!

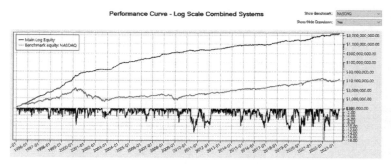

Figure 5.2: Performance of the total suite including the short system.

CHAPTER 5: DO YOU WANT TO SEE EVEN CRAZIER RETURNS?

Here are the amazing results:

- CAGR: 40.38%
- Maximum Drawdown: 18.26%
- Maximum Duration of the Drawdown: around 0.8 years

Crazy, huh?

So, what we did is we gave 50% allocation to all suite of long systems of the total equity, and we gave our short system 50% allocation. Do you remember how we used 100% to create our seven-systems curve? This is where we only gave it 50% instead and then we allowed our one Short system to have the other 50%.

Each system in the seven-systems suite is now running at half the allocation, which automatically reduces drawdowns for all the long positions, but our short system works in a non-correlated manner and that boosts our overall curve.

Combined it's 100% allocation, which means that no leverage was used for this test run.

Now, do you dare to compare it to buy-and-hold strategies that we had earlier?

Do you see the power of non-correlated systems?

	NDX Index (ETF) B&H	Nasdaq-100 Only	7-Systems Suite of Systems	Long & Short Suite of Systems
CAGR	13.59%	21.80%	21.52%	**40.38%**
Max Drawdown	82.90%	45.89%	29.98%	**18.26%**
Max Duration of the Drawdown	15.5 years	3.5 years	3.2 years	**0.8 years**

*B&H: Buy and Hold

Table 5.1: Comparison of different systems from 1995 till June 2023.

Drilling Down Further

This might be too exciting for you to handle, and you'll say to yourself, "Man, I'm going to run this myself now!"

It's a big temptation but let me show you a little bit more of the same suite of systems but from a different timeframe.

You might notice that a lot of the curve for this suite of systems comes from earlier years: 1995–2000. There are a lot of factors contributing to this phenomenon, but in most cases, it's related to the fact that commissions were so high back then that not many retail customers were around. So, prices were moving in a much more organized way and with less noise.

Once commission prices came down, retail customers started flooding in on the scene. Also, high-frequency trading was introduced, which also affected how stocks are moving now.

For that reason, when we create systems with all of our students, we concentrate on the starting date of 2007 for these types of Short systems.

This way, we will catch a big financial crisis, and we're testing it in the era of a lot of retail customers and high-frequency trading.

Let me show you how our Long Systems were stacking up from 2007:

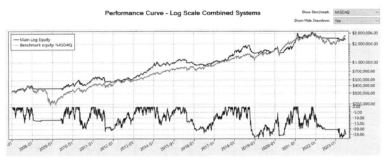

Figure 5.3: Performance of all the Long Systems in our suite from 2007 till June 2023.

Here are the results:

- CAGR: 13.97%
- Maximum Drawdown: 29.96%
- Maximum Duration of the Drawdown: around 2.2 years

And just to put things in perspective, here are the stats for just the NDX index for the same time period (the red benchmark seen on the Figure 5.3):

- CAGR: 13.73%
- Maximum Drawdown: 53.65%
- Maximum Duration of the Drawdown: around 3.2 years

Now, let's add the Short system to the comparison:

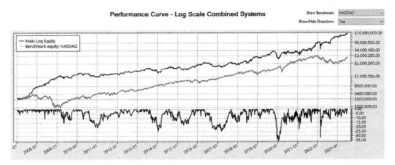

Figure 5.4: Performance of the Short system from 2007 till June 2023.

Here are the results:

- CAGR: 26.45%
- Maximum Drawdown: 35.75%
- Maximum Duration of the Drawdown: around 1.7 years

And now if we put it all together:

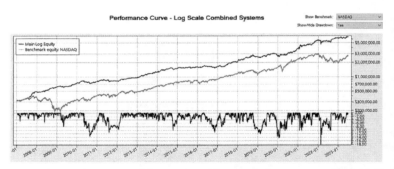

Figure 5.5: Performance of the combined long and short systems from 2007 till June 2023.

Here are the results of the combined suite of systems from 2007:

- CAGR: 21.89%
- Maximum Drawdown: 18.26%

- Maximum Duration of the Drawdown: around 0.8 years

It's still a pretty good result, just not as exciting as we saw from a test from 1995. This is because our long systems are not producing a high CAGR from 2007.

That's why this is just the beginning and not the end result of what you will want to trade live.

	NDX Index (ETF) B&H	Nasdaq-100 Only	7-Systems Suite of Systems	Long & Short Suite of Systems
CAGR	13.73%	13.97%	13.97%	**21.89%**
Max Drawdown	53.65%	45.89%	29.98%	**18.26%**
Max Duration of the Drawdown	15.5 years	3 years	2.2 years	**0.8 years**

*B&H: Buy and Hold

Table 5.2: Comparison of different systems from 2007 till June 2023.

SHORT SYSTEMS:

- There are different types available to use: Contrarian, Go-With-The-Trend, Hedge types.
- If you use Contrarian, you go against the flow. Make sure that you're mentally okay with that and ready to trade Short systems.
- Short systems by definition provide very non-correlated results to Long systems.
- Combining Short and Long systems together produces the best result: highly increased CAGR and highly reduced drawdowns.

CHAPTER 6

Now What Do We Do?

The Work Begins And What You Can Achieve Using Our Three-Step Process

At this stage, we can see we would definitely need to have more Short systems. It will help us smooth things out, and we will need to minimize the corporate risks.

Corporate risks are the risks associated with each individual stock where it can go against us.

Why is it called Corporate Risk? It's quite simple. Each stock is a public company, aka corporation. If this corporation goes down in bankruptcy, then our Long positions will go down to $0. If this corporation has some success and all of a sudden rallies to the sky, then our Short systems will suffer very big losses, in some cases exceeding the investment amount for the position.

We want to protect ourselves from these adverse moves by distributing the equity across different stocks. Our Long systems already have pretty good diversity, but having just one Short system will have a very large exposure to any particular stock.

This is where the grunt work begins. You'd need to start creating more Short systems to make sure our corporate risk is lowered. Plus, as I already mentioned, we will smooth out all those spiky drawdowns.

More Ideas To Use

As we are creating more systems, we can start using more ideas to see which types of systems to create and how to make them non-correlated.

For example, we can look at commodities such as metals – Gold (GLD ETF) and Silver (SLV ETF) – and create a system using these symbols.

Why would we do that? That's because historically we know that metals don't correlate with how stocks move. We can use that to try to patch some of the drawdowns in our curve with the metals' system.

What about Bonds? Bonds are a good choice too. We can create Long and Short systems for Bonds because they are not correlated most of the time to the stocks. Symbols like TLT, BND, JNK, and more would work for that.

You see what I mean? The number of ideas to try and create systems is almost endless.

We will be creating more Short systems, in general, too, using different stock universes or ways of detecting the pullbacks or rallies. It's similar to what we've done with the seven-systems suite of Long systems.

It takes time, but the benefit will definitely outweigh the efforts exerted to create these systems.

Phil's Story – The Three-Step Process To Success

Now, let me tell you a short story about one of our students.

If you talk to Phil, he will admit to you that he knew nothing about indicators, different types of systems, and any of the technical and scary-sounding terminologies.

He was just like me, wondering about how to protect his money when market conditions change all the time and how to increase his wealth, too, so he could enjoy his early retirement.

He went through different market cycles of boom and bust and saw his equity going down by 50% or more at some point. That's where he said, "It was one of the scariest moments for me to see all the money just melting away without any way of stopping it!"

When he joined our group, it was ask-the-questions time!

Boy, he had a lot of questions, but there are no bad questions to ask ever! That's the beauty of this: you will never stop learning, and there is always some new and exciting way of unlocking this mystery.

Our calls would go like this:

- "Alexei, how do I reduce the drawdowns?"
- Or, "Alexei, what do I need to do to create a different system type?"
- Or, "Laurens, what do I need to think about when creating a system?"
- And much more.

All of these questions were revolving around the Three-Step process that I can outline in a nutshell below:

- **Step #1,** you must realize you need to create a system, which is a set of rules. We've talked about it already, but **the most important part is you need to create a SIMPLE system**. A simple system means you don't create a system that will try to handle different market conditions, but rather have a system that will work only in the cases that you're looking for. As an example, it has to go up a lot when it's a bull market. But we would know if the market turns south, then the system would most likely start losing too. This is normal and expected of this system. I know it may sound strange and scary to accept the fact the system would be losing money, but that is the interesting part of this game: we don't need to try to fix this system, we will just come up with another system that does work during that time.
- **Step #2,** which leads us to a realization that we need to create non-correlated systems to succeed. That's how they will start helping each other and will smooth out all the drawdowns and boost our compounded

returns. Different non-correlated systems would work for different market conditions, such as down, up, and sideways markets.

- **Step #3,** and the most crucial step that people don't understand right away, is you need to create these systems that you (and only you!) like and understand. You have full confidence when they work; and when they fail, you know that it's the way it is, and that some other system is stepping in to help this one out. If you take this step and you do it right, you're set for a successful Suite of Systems. You would not doubt your systems. You would not think too much about whether you should be in a position or should not. You would not override your system's process and sabotage yourself.

Phil followed through this process, step-by-step and system-by-system. He went through a lot of testing and then testing some more. He asked a lot of questions and did a lot of thinking too. He evolved to be at the top of this game and arrived at the end of our journey with the following equity curve and statistics that he's gladly allowed me to share with all of you.

As he was developing his suite of systems, he did realize several times that the more you look at it, and the more you learn, the better you become. That's where he had to revise his earlier systems to make sure that he followed Step #3 above and improved his suite even more.

This journey never ends, though. Since there are so many more things to try and do, using the baby steps approach is much more beneficial than one giant grand opening.

Here is Phil's equity graph from 2007:

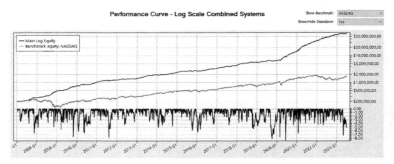

Figure 6.1: Performance equity curve from Phil's Suite of Systems from 2007 till June 2023.

And amazing statistics:

- CAGR: 41.61%
- Maximum Drawdown: 8.64%
- Maximum Duration of the Drawdown: five months

He has 25 systems as of this writing. (And I know that he's already working on a lot more systems. The fun never stops!)

There are Long Trend Following systems, Mean Reversion Long and Mean Reversion Short systems, Hedge Short systems, Inflation-fighting Commodity and Bonds systems, and even Fear Index (VIX) fighting systems.

Once again, he knew nothing about systematic trading when he started and then evolved into this beast mode professional trader all within a few months span!

All the while, he is not sitting in front of the charts all day and sweating profusely by the tug of war of his emotions – *Should I place an order or should I not?* He is now trading this exact suite live in an automatic fashion and continues developing more systems in his leisure time.

And to finish this with a graph from 1995, just so you can see that even running it from the earlier days, his suite is quite a beauty to watch.

He has designed the suite for a lot of systems from 2007, so seeing it perform well in what is called the out-of-sample period is quite nice!

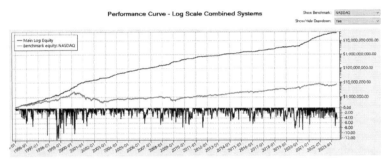

Figure 6.2: Performance equity curve from Phil's Suite of Systems from 1995 till June 2023.

And the statistics:

- CAGR: 53.65%
- Maximum Drawdown: 12.93%
- Maximum Duration of the Drawdown: five months

This is such an amazing result! He's achieved it in less than four months of systems development too: from 0 knowledge to this full suite of systems.

This is not exactly a typical result, though, but close enough to represent what the majority of our students create. Each student has their own ideas and ways they gravitate to one or another style of a system. As the saying goes: there are as many trading ideas as there are trades in the market!

GRUNT WORK PAYS OFF:

- Continue developing new systems for the suite, and you'll smooth out your drawdowns and improve your CAGR along the way.
- It's possible to achieve very good results in a short period of time. Yes, it will be a lot of work during that time, but then you'll reap the results going forward.

CHAPTER 7

What To Know
When Developing Systems

Different Types Of Systems

I can go on forever on the intricacies of different styles and ways of handling systems development, but here is my generic take for what kind of systems you can work on at the base level:

- Long-Term Trend Following systems
- Mean Reversion Long and Mean Reversion Short systems
- Hedge Short systems
- Inflation Commodities and Bonds systems

Most of these systems are what you've heard of in other books, even used by discretionary traders. This is normal, and most likely you can come up with more variations of them, but the essence stays the same.

Don't get me wrong, it may feel like that whatever system you've read about sounds like it's something entirely different, but it's almost always coming back to the same general idea:

- You follow the trend for as long as you can.
- Or you are trying to revert to some kind of equilibrium state, which is called a mean (average state or direction).

The difference is how you achieve these two things and how you can move back and forth between these types of overall systems.

Let's review a little bit in more detail each type so you can decide which ones you gravitate toward more and which ones you want to include in your suite of systems.

Long-Term Trend Following Systems

Take a look at the chart below and you can draw a graph of what the price does for the stock.

It goes up or it goes down, or maybe it's moving sideways.

It can't do anything else, other than just go to $0 and stay there if the stock was delisted from the exchange or declared bankrupt or go higher and higher.

Figure 7.1: This is what AAPL stock looks like in the most recent history in a weekly bar chart.

What if we try to get into a position and stay with the trend as it goes up for as long as it's still going up? That's the basic premise of the Trend Following approach.

The trend can be short-lived or can be long-lived. It's all relative to the timeframe you choose. If you choose a daily timeframe, then some trends can be long, and some can be short in duration there. But, if you switch to the one-minute bar timeframe for the same stock, then the same "short duration" trend suddenly becomes quite long:

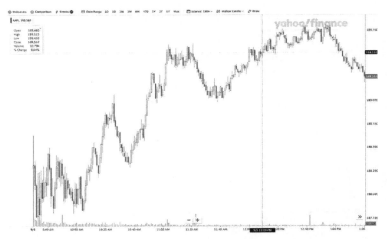

Figure 7.2: One-minute bar chart graph for AAPL on September 5, 2023. You can see trends throughout the day.

Trends are always present in all stocks. It's just a matter of duration for the chosen timeframe and the amplitude (how big it is in terms of the price change).

We can capitalize on this knowledge and come up with systems where we try to stay with the chosen trend.

How would we do that? Well, this is exactly what we did in all of our Long systems earlier in the book. We sorted stocks over a longer timeframe by ranking with our Highest Rate of Change of 252 days stocks to get into. This was done for a reason: choose trending stocks, get into them, and then stay there for as long as we can. In our case, "as long as we can" translated into a set of Exit rules where we used a Trailing Stop.

Trailing was one of the available mechanisms to stay with the trend. It's not the only mechanism, though. We can do the same using other ways of "staying with the trend."

One example of trailing the stock is using moving averages as our exit price. Moving average, by definition, is a smoothing mechanism, which means that as it averages the price, it will lag behind and it does provide us with useful information on seeing if our trend is ending.

It's one of the classical ways of trailing and we can use it instead of using a percentage trailing stop.

All of the above methods are using indicators to see how we can stay with the trend. This is what we normally refer to as Technical Exits. There are a lot of different technical exits that can be used. Some of them are indicators like:

- Donchian Channel – hitting Lowest Low in X days for a Long type of system
- Keltner Channel – classical Exponential Moving Average and ATR channel
- Bollinger Band – classical Simple Moving Average and Standard Deviation channel

And many more that can be used for this exit type.

The key to it all is to remember: *we're trying to stay with the trend for as long as we can.*

I know, I keep repeating it like mantra, but this part is so important that people might not realize this is the true essence of the Trend Following system.

It's not so much about Entries and rather mostly about Exits.

You can randomly enter into a position for a stock, then follow it with the Trailing Stop of your choice, and then actually have a winning trade!

That's why Exits is the key to Trend Following.

What it also means, since we're trend following "for as long as we can," we pretty much never exit at a profit when the stock is right at the very top of its price move.

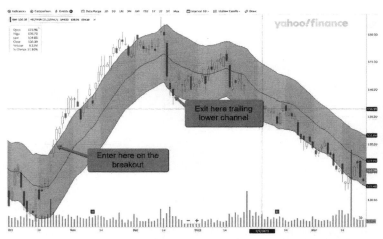

Figure 7.3: Keltner technical exit in action where, on a daily chart, it will exit when we dip below the lower band of the channel.

In the graph above, you can see multiple opportunities to get into positions and then trend follow with a Keltner Channel for a profit. Every time the price was going above the channel, we could enter into a position, and then once we dip below the lower channel boundary, we will exit.

Some positions on the same graph would have been losing positions too. That's why this is not a guarantee of winning a trade and rather a methodology of trend following.

We will never exit at the top of the move though using this approach if all we do is follow the trend using some kind of trailing.

Think about it for a second. How would we know that we're hitting a top? We can try to predict the top with oscillator-based indicators, such as RSI, where it gives us an idea that we're possibly getting into an overbought territory. Would it be enough to rely on this though? Probably a good thing to try, but again, if you want to stay with the trend for as long as you can, you might want to weed out any noise in the price movements. Using just RSI will not allow you to do just that, so you'd need to have an additional way of handling it.

Trailing stop is the reliable way of making sure that we're avoiding unnecessary noise and staying with the trend while it's still there.

Now, you should start getting an idea why, if you're using a trend following approach, even though you have a profitable system, you will have drawdowns.

The drawdowns appear when the stock either immediately goes down once we got into a position and hits our protective stop. Or we trailed it, and then when the trend ended, it hit our trailing stop, which gave up some of the unrealized profits before allowing us to get stopped out.

We can't trail the price too tightly though, because we will be prematurely stopped out due to the noise in the price of the stock.

We can't trail too wide either, because then we give up too much in profits. It's a balance, like Goldilocks – "just right."

See the way now how it works?

Why, then, do you see so many different books and systems on the internet telling you to "buy low, sell high," or "buy a dip," or have a "risk to reward ratio of at least 1:2," etc.?

What do you see in common with all these systems? I hope you can start recognizing the general theme there:

"Buy low – sell high." Isn't it what trend following does? You buy low and sell high by following the trend. You just never sell at the *highest point* most likely, but you're still following the trend.

"Buy a dip." – this one is a little controversial because I can use the same approach as in our next system type (Mean Reversion Long). However, for the sake of this discussion, we can now clearly imagine that if you buy a dip, then you're trying to at least expect the stock to go up, and you're holding on to it "for as long as you can." So, it still can be interpreted as a type of trend following.

Risk to reward ratio at least 1:2, or some number like that. The whole idea here is to expect a stock to go up in price (trending stock). You get in to risk some amount of money, but hoping the price will go up at least 2x more than what you're risking in this example of a 1:2 risk-to-reward ratio. It's a trend-following approach, too, because you're trying to anticipate the trend and make sure that you get out before it ends without any trailing of the price, but hoping to hit that top.

When we're developing Trend Following systems, we can use any of the above techniques to craft the system.

Moreover, I'd say that in some cases, we must start using different techniques to create a variety of systems, so that we don't try to get into the same stocks.

I've already touched on this topic before, but briefly, it's needed, so that we don't experience a corporate risk in our systems where a stock can go down to $0 in price if the company goes bankrupt.

Now, we're mostly using the trend-following technique for Long-Term Trend Following systems. The keywords here are "Long-Term," meaning that we aim to stay with the trend on a long-term basis. The reason for this is that what we're looking for is the following scenario:

- We might get stopped out at a loss, but the loss is small.
- But when we win, we win really big.

This is what is called a **positive skew system**. If we put all our losses and wins on a graph as a histogram, then the biggest wins will be all the way to the right, and all the small losses are evenly distributed in that histogram.

This type of system thrives on the old adage: "Cut the losses short and let the winners run." In some cases, the Win/Loss ratio becomes quite extreme in these types of systems. Seeing a 10:1 or 15:1 ratio is normal. This means for every $1 lost, you win $10 or $15, respectively. What it also means is that the Win Percentage (Win%) is always less than 50%. In those extreme cases, it can be 20%. Meaning you lose 80% of the time, but when you win, you win big, but only 20% of the time.

For a lot of people, it's a hard pill to swallow.

Imagine running that type of a system and every day you place an order.

You get into a position, and then you're stopped out on a stop loss.

Then you do it again, and again, and again.

You're still stopped out.

You'll be so tempted to just give up at some point and say, "Okay, I'm not placing this trade." But the problem is, what if that trade turned into that big win that you're waiting for?

Do you see now that having a systematic approach to this and not using your emotions is going to be so much more beneficial?

That's why so many discretionary traders don't go for a classical trend-following strategy. It's so hard to run it physically and emotionally! They opt for the already-discussed "risk to reward ratio" types, because it's much easier to handle mentally and emotionally, and you can see and visualize your reward too, since you'll have your Profit Target order there.

Mean Reversion Long Systems

Now, let's review a different beast, which can be even more controversial and sometimes harder to trade too.

"Mean Reversion" refers to the fact that a price might have some equilibrium and any deviation from that state will cause the price to come back to it.

In the case of a Long system, that means the very infamous expression "buy the dip." It's infamous, in my opinion, because this expression doesn't really clarify why I need to buy the dip and, most importantly, when do I need to do it.

If you think of the trend as your equilibrium direction, then it's easy to understand what the mean reversion is supposed to be doing. Meaning, if the price keeps climbing up, but sometimes it can go down temporarily to what we would then consider "a dip," then it makes sense to buy the stock at that point, expecting it to climb back up to the prevailing trend direction.

This sounds nice and perfectly logical, but the issue with this is knowing two things: 1) what's the prevailing direction, and 2) when is this temporary dip trying to revert to the mean?

How do we know both of these things?

Ever heard of a "catching a falling knife" problem? This is when a trader tries to buy a falling stock, thinking that they are buying "a dip," but unfortunately, the stock doesn't stop falling and causes big losses.

Nobody likes this idea, and that's why it becomes controversial to have Mean Reversion systems. They are, by definition, contrarian in approach.

What we're trying to do is to capitalize on these dips, but doing it so that we're not constantly catching falling knives for Mean Reversion Long systems. In other words, *contrarian* would mean we're doing the opposite of what the majority of participants are doing.

How do we, then, figure it out? How do we know when the dip is a dip to buy for a Long system and when it's not a good idea to do?

The answer is straightforward: *you never know, but at least you can statistically confirm if there is an edge in what you're doing.*

We can confirm it using different methods:

- *Using oscillators, such as Connors RSI, RSI, Money Flow Index, and others.* What they all have in common is the ability to give us an idea if the stock is in an oversold or overbought condition. It doesn't mean it predicts it all the time, it only gives us an indication of this fact, which we can use.

- *Using different other means of figuring out we're in a temporary dip, also known as a pullback.* We can use things like moving averages, the number of down days in a row, and/or percentage of the size of the dip. All of this allows us to quantify the dip. Again, it won't be perfect, but we're not looking for perfection here.

Take a look at the graph below of Apple stock (AAPL) on a daily chart with nine-days Exponential Moving Average pullbacks. As you can see, while the trend was still going up, there were plenty of opportunities to buy the dip and revert back to the main trend, aka mean, to reap the profits.

Figure 7.4: AAPL stock with the main trend going up and pullbacks to nine-days EMA.

This is a very typical scenario we're looking for in our Mean Reversion strategy for the Long side.

One thing we still haven't answered yet, though, is how do we know which way the trend is going, and we can consider our dip being "the dip"?

There is an easy solution to it.

We can measure the trend via a lot of different ways.

Here are a few that you might already know and can guess, but there are also some that might be a little puzzling to you, which is normal, and that's why I'm here to show you the possibilities.

Using Longer-term Moving Averages, Such As A 200-days EMA (Exponential Moving Average)

Figure 7.5: Trend is up while our stock is above the 200-days EMA for AAPL.

Here is the same graph as before, which we saw with nine-days EMA pullbacks, but now with 200-days EMA plotted on it.

You can see that sometimes the stock is below it and sometimes above it.

In our case, we can have a rule, which will tell us that if the price of the stock is above 200-days EMA, then the general trend is Up. That means that now we will be trying to buy the dips (pullbacks to nine-days EMA). Otherwise, if the price of the stock is below the 200-days EMA, then we won't be buying anything because we don't know if the pullbacks are actually the dips.

Let me show you what this system would look like on the Healthcare Sector (I just randomly chose it because I know that there are lot of high-flying stocks in that sector, and we need stocks to move for this to work.):

This system has the following rules:

- Healthcare Sector stocks
- We choose ten positions at any given point to get into.
- We use 2% Fixed Risk position sizing.
- We only trade stocks that are at least $1 or more in price.
- We only trade stocks that have at least $500,000 dollar volume per day over an average of 20 days period.
- We only trade stocks that have an ATR% greater than 1% and less than 40%.
- We only trade stocks that are trending above 200-day EMA (our trend indicator).
- We only trade stocks that have ADX of seven days greater than 35 (our strength of the move).
- We're looking for a stock that pulled back to nine-days EMA and its price below it right now.

- We're looking for a stock that has had at least two subsequent down days.
- We will sort (rank) all candidates by Lowest RSI of three days.
- We will trade this stock only as a Limit order of 3% below the previous day's close price.
- We will exit at a Stop Loss of two ATRs over ten days.
- Or we will exit at the Profit Target of 5% and it will be triggered intraday.
- Or we will exit on the fourth day if no profit target or a stop loss was hit. *This is needed so that we don't sit in an unprofitable trade forever. Mean Reversion systems rely on higher trade frequency to generate profits.*

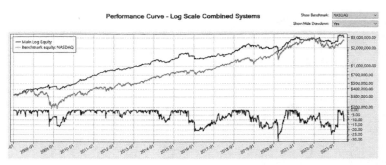

Figure 7.6: Performance curve of the nine-days pullback MR Long system from 2007 till June 2023.

Here are the statistics for this system:

- CAGR: 14.82%
- Maximum Drawdown: 30.35%
- Maximum Duration of the Drawdown: around 2.3 years

And here is the kicker. What if we decided to use five-days EMA instead of our original nine-days?

Here are the statistics for this system (Figure 7.7 below):

- CAGR: 19.25%
- Maximum Drawdown: 28.97%
- Maximum Duration of the Drawdown: around 2.3 years

See what I mean about this type of pullback? I've tested out different EMAs and five-days, in this particular case, seems to be a stable choice given the way these trades work for this stock universe.

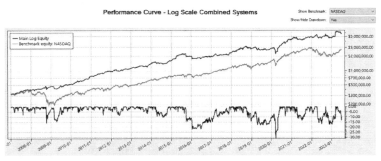

Figure 7.7: Performance curve of the five-days pullback MR Long system from 2007 till June 2023.

Another Way Of Measuring A Trend Is Via The Longer-term RSI

What if we're looking for a stock that has a long-term oscillator telling us that it's not really in a downtrend.

RSI tells us if we're in an oversold or overbought condition. The typical values for that are: if it's below 20, then we're in an oversold condition, and if it's above 80, then it's in an overbought condition.

Here is the same system that we've compiled above, but now instead of having a 200-days EMA for Trend identification, we will substitute it with RSI of 100 days and value must be above 40. That means we're not in the oversold condition and sort of closer to the middle of the line. I bet you that you don't see this often in books used as a trend indicator. (I haven't seen it even once so far used for that purpose, so let me know of a book that you've read when they used it like this!)

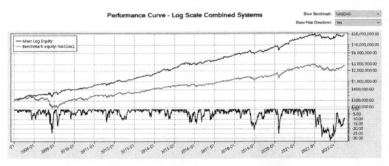

Figure 7.8: Performance curve of a five-days EMA pullback and 100 days RSI over 40 threshold for Trend from 2007 till June 2023.

Here are the statistics for this system:

- CAGR: 28.81%
- Maximum Drawdown: 37.49%
- Maximum Duration of the Drawdown: around 1.5 years

Crazy, huh? Well, don't get way too excited about it because when I've tested this system rules on other stock universes, they were not as good, so it was some sheer luck that got me here. Yet, it shows you that there are ways of measuring things more than one way for sure. Also, we will go over testing systems for robustness, and you'll see how the settings and results relate to each other.

And Yet Another Way Of Measuring The Trend Is Via Percent Return

It's the same as Rate of Change that we've used for our ranking, but now we can be more explicit and tell the system that we're looking for stocks that rallied in, let's say, 200 days for more than 20%.

I just randomly chose 20% at this point and might as well experiment with other versions, but let's see what will happen if we replace RSI 100 days above with Percent Return greater than 20%:

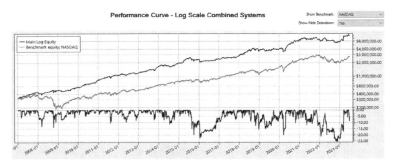

Figure 7.9: Performance curve of a five-days EMA pullback and percent Return over 200 days and greater than 20% for Trend from 2007 till June 2023.

Here are the statistics for this system:

- CAGR: 22.15%
- Maximum Drawdown: 27.41%
- Maximum Duration of the Drawdown: around 1.6 years

It's a pretty good system, as you can see, and it's all about figuring out how to make sure that we "buy the dip" only when it makes sense with our trend indicator usage.

Another very important point here is, if you look closely, you'll notice how this system behaves even in times of Financial Crisis or other times when typical Long-Term Trend Following systems would fail while this one would still work.

This again leads us to the most important point I've already mentioned several times by now that you should recognize and just print it out, put it right next to your monitor, and repeat daily:

You're looking for non-correlated systems to make sure that you protect and build your wealth in the down, up, and sideways markets!!!

If I keep building more and more non-correlated systems, I will make my curve look more and more like what you saw from Phil. This is exactly what Phil and others do in our group and so should you!

Regardless whether you decide to create your own systems the way I'm showing you here or any other way, just make sure that you do it in a way where these systems are non-correlated. You'll see the difference – 100% guaranteed!

We can go into more and more different ways of measuring the Trend, but you should now get the point of how to use it to your advantage.

Let's switch to Mean Reversion Short now.

Mean Reversion Short Systems

We have already seen and used this one earlier in the book when we constructed the Short System for our Suite of Systems.

Mean Reversion (MR) Short systems have similar characteristics like Mean Reversion Long, but the only major difference is that most times we don't want to use any kind of Trend Filter to disallow getting into stocks.

Unlike in our example for Mean Reversion Long where we used different styles of Trend identification, we're trying to be more encompassing for the Mean Reversion Short here and instead letting them all in.

This is because, as discussed before, we can be either Contrarian in nature or Go-With-The-Trend in nature. Contrarian works much more reliably in the tests that I've done to date, so if you look back at the Chapter 5 Contrarian Short System that we created, you'll see now quite a familiar setup:

- There is a stock universe chosen.
- We filter our stocks by price and volume.

- We filter our stocks by ATR% volatility.
- We test the strength of the moves with the ADX.
- We test the pullback.
- We rank the stocks.
- We have an order type, most of the time it would be a Limit order.
- We have a stop loss defined.
- We also possibly have other exits defined, such as profit targets.
- We have a timed exit defined.

All of this is quite typical for Mean Reversion Short or Long systems.

This always comes back to the choices you make for each setup when you create a new Mean Reversion Short system. Sometimes you don't even use ADX for strength, and sometimes you do. In some cases, you use RSI as a pullback and in other cases you use EMA as your pullback, or some other pullback.

It's not rocket science, but it does become tedious, and you definitely need to experiment a lot to test your different ideas.

An entire book can be written going into different pullbacks and logic behind them. Or what stock universe to use and how to use them.

What Are The Differences In Long-Term Trend Versus Mean Reversion Systems?

So far, we've clearly established what Long-Term Trend Following systems do and how they generate drawdowns. What about Mean Reversions?

Mean Reversion systems operate on a much smaller scale. What it means is that the moves are much smaller in nature since we're trying to catch the pullback and then wait until we're safely back to the mean and we can get out with a profit.

The stop loss is tighter because our moves are tighter. That's why we normally don't even need to trail the stop loss since we're just looking for a way to return to the mean.

With all that said, what we're trying to accomplish here is to generate a system, which is **a neutral skew system**.

A neutral skew would mean that our losses are similar in size as compared to our wins, but we do have more wins versus losses.

We're looking for higher than 50% Win Percentage and our Win/Loss Ratio is normally closer to one, sometimes can even be below one but not too far. When Win/Loss Ratio is below one, that would mean that for every dollar we win, we lose more than we won.

As an example, the Mean Reversion Long system with Percent Return for Trend has Win% of 63.51% and Win/Loss Ratio of 0.75. So, for every 75 cents won we are losing $1 but since we're winning 63.51% of the time, we're winning with this system.

That's the key difference between Long Term Trend Following systems versus Mean Reversion systems. In Long-Term Trend Following we're waiting for our big win and incur a lot of small losses, but in Mean Reversion style we're looking for a lot of small wins by outnumbering small losses.

This makes all these Mean Reversion systems quite sensitive to the changes in the market conditions. When the market changes for whatever reason, such as high frequency trading comes in, or something else affected it, then it may alter the performance of the mean reversion system a lot.

When it's a Long-Term Trend Following system, because it lives off of those big wins, usually these same market changes don't alter the performance too much, which makes Long-Term Trend Following systems much more reliable at their performance on the long-term basis.

Hedge Protection Systems

Hedge protection systems are designed to provide protection to the whole or part of the suite of systems when the market changes direction suddenly. A good recent example is the COVID-19 crash of the market.

The market was going down several days in a row, and it looked like there was no stopping it.

None of your Long-Term Trend Following (LTTF) Systems would work at that point and they would go down too along with the market.

Your Mean Reversion Long systems would suddenly just keep catching falling knives because none of the pullbacks are temporary. It's just the overall trend is still pointing up because it's lagging behind due to its longer-term nature. That means all your Mean Reversion Long systems would be generating big drawdowns right along with your Long-Term Trend Following Long systems.

Your Mean Reversion Short systems would not even be engaging. This is because of the way their Order Entry portion is set up. Remember that in most cases it uses a Limit order? Well, normally it would mean that the stock must go up enough during the day to trigger that limit order but now, when the market is dropping like a stone, every day all stocks just gap down beyond the Limit order price. This means that no orders will be triggered.

Panic is in the market and none of your systems would be working and generating any protection. Moreover, all of your stocks related to Long systems would become correlated. They go in a lockstep downward march that would seem endless and painful.

The solution is to have protection systems that are designed to make sure that in that kind of panic environment they get in and soften that blow that is coming from all these Long systems.

These systems behave like an insurance policy for your Suite of Systems. They don't look pretty but they are designed to work when panic sets in.

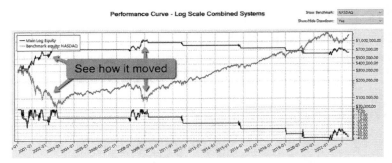

Figure 7.10: Performance curve of a Nasdaq-100 index based hedge protection system from 2000 till June 2023.

As you see, it's not making much money by itself, but it works when there is a big market panic, i.e., early 2000s and 2008 financial crises, COVID-19, 2022 bear market.

For this system, the rules were simple:

- We use QQQ ETF as our Nasdaq-100 index substitute.
- We wait if our current price of QQQ is trading below 25 days EMA and 7% below that EMA.
- Then we enter as a Market On Open order.
- And stay there trailing 25% behind.
- And our initial stop loss order is five ATR of 100 days for ATR.

Other Systems

At this point, we can now start creating different systems to complement our Suite of Systems.

We can target different commodities and bonds to create systems as non-correlated to stocks. This could be done as an example on GLD ETF for gold.

This is a simple GLD type of a system:

- GLD as our instrument we're working with.
- We enter only into one full position at a time and allocate full equity to this position.
- We would enter if the price of GLD is above the highest high of the last 50 days.
- We enter as a Market On Open order type.
- We would exit when the price of GLD is below the lowest low of the last 100 days.

This is the whole system. It's very simple and the point of it is not to generate a high CAGR but rather to work as a non-correlated system for our stock-related long systems.

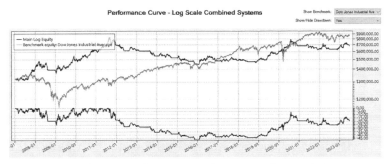

Figure 7.11: Performance of GLD system from 2007 till June 2023 using Dow Jones Industrials index as a benchmark.

I've deliberately put Dow Jones Industrials index as a benchmark so that it's easier to see for comparison how this system works.

You can see it works in most cases in the opposite direction to what our benchmark is doing. This is exactly what we're looking for in this case.

SYSTEM DEVELOPMENT POINTS:

- Generally different types of systems exist: Long-Term Trend Following (LTTF), Mean Reversion (MR) Long, and Mean Reversion (MR) Short.
- LTTF systems use various methods to determine the Trend direction.
- LTTF systems have a Positive Skew, relying on big wins and incurring many small losses.
- Mean Reversion systems operate differently, focusing on smaller moves, and are Skew Neutral, aiming for a higher quantity of small wins compared to small losses.
- Knowing what you're trying to accomplish will help you choose which system type is more appropriate for the job.
- Hedge protection and other systems can mitigate drawdowns and provide relief during market downturns.

CHAPTER 8

What Else Is Important For System Development?

Robustness Testing

In all the systems that we've created so far, we have not really figured out one important aspect: are they robust or not? How would we know if we picked the parameters that would produce reliable results going forward?

The unfortunate answer is we wouldn't know. We would still be guessing, but at least there are ways for us to see if we can make it easier to trust our systems.

This is what we will do: we will run our newly created systems through robustness testing. There are some discretionary ways of doing robustness testing and some that we came up with to automatically test things out.

When we're developing a system, and choosing values for our parameters, we should not try to find the exact best performing value. I've already mentioned this in earlier chapters, but it wouldn't hurt to repeat again.

This is because when we're testing our parameter values, we always use past data and it's very easy to bypass all the known landmines to generate good returns. This is how you'd fool yourself and think you have a very good system, while it's not going to be generating any of the same returns once it's subjected to the live testing.

Some software packages have exactly this functionality where you can click the "optimize" button and it creates the best performing values for your parameters. This is so dangerous that people don't really understand you will lose money by going this route.

What I do, instead, is trying to find the set of values that generate similar results. The results are not the same but are within the ballpark of the performance I'm looking for. I understand this does come with practice and a lot of experience, but it surely does work much better this way versus the "optimize" button approach.

In our examples so far, that was the approach used to choose the parameters and its values. That's why you see a lot of times things like 25% trailing stop or 20% stop loss. The round looking numbers are represented there because they fit the general number within the ballpark of the performance returns I'm looking for each system.

How else can we test to see if the system is robust? There are several things that can be done:

- We can test the same system for different historical data or even, what is called, forward testing too. What it means is we design a system for a wide range of historical data but then when we want to test robustness of it, we widen that range. Some people deliberately let their systems run in a simulation mode for three-to-six months or more after they have been developed, which is sometimes called an *incubation period*. I'm personally not really a fan of it but this could be just me.

- We can run the same system against different sets of stocks to see if we get similar results. However, this can be slightly subjective since we may need to adjust some parameters of the system to make it applicable for the chosen stock universe.

- We can simulate various conditions under which we don't get into the same stocks. This could involve deliberately skipping our best candidates, modifying the closing price for each trading day, or getting into a much larger number of positions to study the statistical effect of diversification of results.

Let's dive in a little bit more to see how this can affect our systems.

Wider Historical Data Testing

Let's take our original Nasdaq-100 system. For simplicity's sake, I'm going to show the equity curve of it here again:

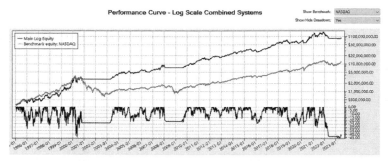

Figure 8.1: Performance curve of our Nasdaq-100 LTTF long system from 1995 till June 2023.

Here are the statistics for this system:

- CAGR: 21.80%
- Maximum Drawdown: 45.89%
- Maximum Duration of the Drawdown: around 3.5 years

Once again, it does look like a good system.

What if we now run it from earlier years with an end date in 2007 instead?

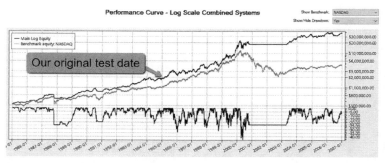

Figure 8.2: Performance curve of the same Nasdaq-100 LTTF Long system from 1985 till January 1st, 2007.

As you can see, this system still holds up pretty nicely with no surprising drawdowns or surges of equity. This is exactly what we are looking for in this test.

Different Stock Universe Testing

How about we run this same system on a different stock universe? If we're planning on doing that, we need to ensure this system has valid stocks for our universe.

Recall that this system is designed for the Nasdaq-100 stocks, which consists of 100 very liquid stocks, none of which are below $1. So, if we're testing the rest of the rules on a different stock universe, we would need to make sure that we get into liquid stocks priced at least $1 or more.

We haven't tried this system on Russell 1000 yet. Let's see what would happen:

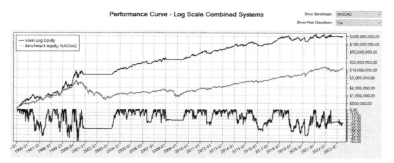

Figure 8.3: Performance curve of Russell 1000 stock universe for the same rules from the Nasdaq-100 LTTF Long system from 1995 till June 2023.

Here are the statistics for this system:

- CAGR: 25.19%
- Maximum Drawdown: 50.30%
- Maximum Duration of the Drawdown: around 3.5 years

This system appears to be performing similarly to the Nasdaq-100 system. Once again, this confirms that the chosen rules are quite robust.

So far so good! Let's see what else we can do to test it further.

Deliberately Skipping Best Candidates

Now, this one is much harder to do manually, but what we're trying to do here is to skip our best candidates.

What does "best candidates" mean?

Remember the rules for the system where we ranked our candidates by the Highest Rate Of Change over 252 days? Those are what we consider the "best candidates."

These are the stocks which have the highest rate of return in the last 252 trading days, and we sorted these candidates in descending order: from the highest to lowest rate of return. This way our best candidates are on the top and worse candidates are on the bottom of the list.

Now, what will happen if we skip the top X-number of stocks? Why do we want to know that? The answer is simple: we want to learn what our system will do if we couldn't get into the top candidates. We want to know if our system still has the edge, and its performance hasn't degraded to the point where we can't even recognize the results.

Obviously, this is just a simulation of "what would happen" type, and yet, it provides quite a powerful view into what our system is capable of. It will give us more confidence that in the future our system will still operate even in the not-so-good conditions.

For this test, we can try to skip different number of top candidates, and for this example let's skip 20% of them and see what will happen to our curve and statistics:

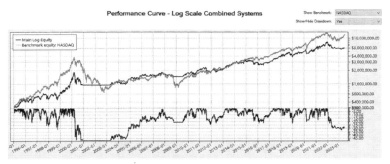

Figure 8.4: Performance curve of the Nasdaq-100 LTTF Long system with skipped 20% of Highest Rate of Change candidates from 1995 till June 2023.

Oh no, something is off now! Take a look at the statistics:

- CAGR: 10.92%
- Maximum Drawdown: 48.55%
- Maximum Duration of the Drawdown: around ten years

Well, now you can see the true face of this system! It was trying to hide its face from us this whole time, but we've uncovered it!

WEALTH WELL-MANAGED

How would I interpret these results? For LTTF Long systems, we should not see such a drastic degradation of results. Which means that with the given parameters (rules), this system would probably operate at this level going forward. It doesn't mean it's a guarantee to behave that way, but at least if you want to be more conservative with your approach, you can assume this is what you'll get.

Now, let's review the rules for it and see what we're missing and why it's degrading so much:

- We use Nasdaq-100 stock set as our stock universe.
- We will enter into ten positions at 10% allocation each. The position sizing here is a simple Percent Size.
- We use Market Filter to not let us get into any new position if price of the NDX index is below SMA (Simple Moving Average) 252 days.
- We will choose the Highest Rate of Change stocks over 252 days.
- We enter as a Market On Open order.
- Our initial Stop Loss is 20%.
- Our Trailing Stop is 20%.

The rules for the system are simple, as we've designed it.

However, we're missing one simple thing. We don't know if these stocks, which have the Highest Rate of Change, are trending Up or Down. They might have generated the highest rate of change in the last 252 days, but the stock might already be going down, and we're not taking this fact into account.

174

Remember how we discussed identifying the Trend for a stock? We can use this same exact technique here. Let's use EMA 100 days to identify if the stock is trending up still.

Here is what the curve of this system looks like if we add EMA 100 days in our Trend section:

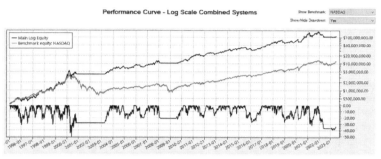

Figure 8.5: Performance curve of the Nasdaq-100 LTTF Long system with the EMA 100 days trend filter included from 1995 till June 2023. No robustness testing performed yet.

Here are the statistics:

- CAGR: 22.78%
- Maximum Drawdown: 50.83%
- Maximum Duration of the Drawdown: around 3.5 years

This is quite comparable to the system without the EMA 100 days from Figure 8.1. The drawdowns are slightly bigger, but so is the CAGR.

Now, let's subject it to the same robustness test of removing 20% of the best ranking candidates:

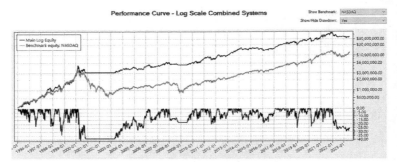

Figure 8.6: Performance curve of the Nasdaq-100 LTTF Long system with the EMA 100 days and robustness 20% skip best ranking candidates.

Here are the statistics:

- CAGR: 17.90%
- Maximum Drawdown: 41.24%
- Maximum Duration of the Drawdown: around 6.1 years

Surprisingly, the drawdowns went down, but the CAGR also decreased somewhat. However, the CAGR didn't decline as much as in our first 20% skip candidates test, which is quite a good thing because most likely this version of the system will operate in a similar way in the future too. This is exactly what we were looking for and confirming with our robustness testing.

Robustness testing has revealed to us that we were actually missing some of the important ingredients for our system. If we had run it as is before we've included the EMA 100 trend filter, we might have wondered why it was not operating as originally designed, all because we didn't consider we had more "luck" versus "edge" on our side. The goal is to have more edge, of course, and we can't just rely on and quantify luck.

Deliberately Getting Into More Positions

Now, let's explore what happens if we deliberately get into 20 positions instead of ten positions at a time.

This way, we will test the system on a much wider range of stocks:

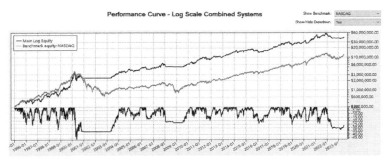

Figure 8.7: Performance curve of the Nasdaq-100 LTTF Long system with the EMA 100 days and doubling of positions at any given time.

Here are the statistics:

- CAGR: 18.74%
- Maximum Drawdown: 47.49%
- Maximum Duration of the Drawdown: around four years

You can see that the CAGR is reduced compared to the ten positions at a time system from Figure 8.5, but the drawdowns are also reduced.

Again, this confirms that the system is quite robust, and even when getting into more candidates, comparable results to the original system are achieved.

What Will Happen If We Test Our Mean Reversion Long System?

Remember when I said, "Don't get too excited," about that version of our MR Long system, which used RSI 100 days with a 40 threshold? Let me perform this 20% skip test on it so you can see what I mean.

Here is how it looks without any robustness tests as a refresher, so you don't have leaf through pages to find it:

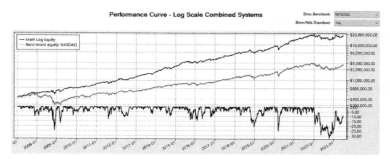

Figure 8.8: Performance curve of the MR Long system with RSI 100 days Trend version without any robustness testing. No robustness testing was performed.

Here are our original statistics without any robustness testing:

- CAGR: 28.79%
- Maximum Drawdown: 37.49%
- Maximum Duration of the Drawdown: around 1.5 years

And here is what will happen to it if we run 20% skip candidates on it:

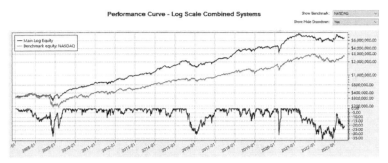

Figure 8.9: Performance curve of the MR Long system with RSI 100 days Trend version and 20% skip candidates robustness test.

Here are the statistics:

- CAGR: 17.10%
- Maximum Drawdown: 37.79%
- Maximum Duration of the Drawdown: around 2.3 years

It's still a decent looking system, but clearly the performance of it has degraded a lot.

For Mean Reversion systems, it's quite common to see this kind of performance degradation during the robustness testing though. This is because Mean Reversion systems operate on much smaller moves, and small changes to parameters and candidates do affect things overall much more compared to Long-Term Trend Long systems.

What if we take a different version of the same system with the Trend filter that we had? How about we pick Percent Return 200 days 20% threshold?

Here is what it looks like without any robustness testing, so we can see how skip candidates will affect it:

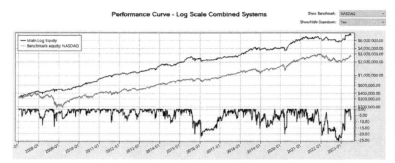

Figure 8.10: Performance curve of the MR Long system with the Percent Return 200 days and 20% threshold for Trend. No robustness testing was performed.

Here are the statistics:

- CAGR: 22.03%
- Maximum Drawdown: 27.41%
- Maximum Duration of the Drawdown: around 1.6 years

And now when we add 20% skip candidates:

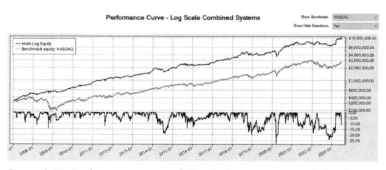

Figure 8.11: Performance curve of the MR Long system with the Percent Return 200 days and 20% threshold for Trend and 20% skip candidates robustness test.

Here are the statistics:

- CAGR: 21.99%
- Maximum Drawdown: 27.87%
- Maximum Duration of the Drawdown: around 1.5 years

It's almost the same system even with the robustness test for it turned on!

That means this version is much more robust for future use compared to the RSI version that we had. However, it doesn't mean we will only use this type of Trend identification in all our other systems. Just keep in mind, we are looking for a variety of systems and especially how they are all combined into a Suite of Systems.

Biggest Sin Using Robustness Testing

Did you notice that in all the above testing I didn't try to optimize my system when I ran my robustness tests? That was done for a reason: we don't want to optimize parameters when we test our systems for robustness to avoid over-optimization.

Doing optimization while testing robustness is cheating and what's the point of this cheating? Are you trying to prove to yourself that you have a very nice-looking equity curve, or that you have a set of systems that will operate reliably in the future? I strongly recommend concentrating on the latter case.

We are not doing it to show to our friends, relatives, and bosses that we have such a very nice curve. We are doing it to make sure that we get to keep and multiply our wealth in any market conditions!

ROBUSTNESS TESTING:

- It's an important step in your system's development. Don't skip it – it will save you a lot of frustration down the road!
- There are different ways of running robustness testing. In some cases, it's an easy way of just expanding the time period or running for a different time period; or by using more positions at a time; or by skipping candidates for each trading day to simulate what would happen to your system; just to name a few.
- A lot more different ways exist to do robustness testing, but we just can't cover them all in this book.
- Avoid the biggest robustness testing sin: Don't try to optimize while testing using robustness testing techniques. It's a sin not worth committing!

CHAPTER 9

Emotions And Systems Development

Are We Immune To Emotions?

No, we're not. If someone tells you that once you have your systems developed and running, you'll be completely immune to any emotions and can put everything on autopilot, they are lying to you.

The unfortunate truth is no systems exist without drawdowns or difficult periods. While we are delighted when systems make money, we also experience worry and self-doubt when they go down.

We are still humans, and we designed these systems with a cool head, looking at a much longer history where years are just blips on the curve. However, in real life, the ups and downs on the curve happen at a much slower pace. We live it one day at a time, and it's not easy to completely disappear for a year or even a few months, leaving our systems to operate on their own and then come back to see the results.

Imagine if you designed your systems, then set it up and let it run, and then disappeared for ten years and then came back to see that you've multiplied your wealth several times over, but there were some bumps along the way.

"Oh, well," you'd say, "I still multiplied my wealth – not a big deal!" Of course, it's not a big deal if you really don't look at what was happening along the way, but can we really not look?

Most likely you will check.

System development is an ongoing process. You'll realize that you could add more systems or use different ways of measuring things. It will be an ever-ongoing improvement, which is quite a good thing. You'll continue not only to improve your suite of systems, but you'll also improve yourself and your way of looking at it.

So, you'd better learn how to deal with this on the emotional level.

Interview With Laurens Bensdorp

I had a call with Laurens where we were discussing how to make sure that our students understand this aspect of systematic trading in which emotions play a very big role.

Alexei: You've been at systematic development for a very long time now. How did it evolve for you?

Laurens: Indeed, I've been doing systematic development for more than 17 years now and things have changed quite a bit.

CHAPTER 9: EMOTIONS AND SYSTEMS DEVELOPMENT

Originally, I was doing just Mean Reversion systems, but then I've realized that the variability of them was very high, and they were affected by the market conditions.

I've started systematic trading when the market was in the bear market of the Dot Com Bust period, and that affected my thinking to use Short systems to make sure I can benefit from the down market.

Later, I've learned along the way to use Long-Term Trend Following systems when the market changed to bull, and that helped me to improve my suite even further.

My main objective was always creating a set of non-correlated systems for any market condition, but my learning process never stopped, even now!

Alexei: That's incredible if you think about it. I've personally started from LTTF Long side of things and did the opposite – learned to have and use Mean Reversion systems in my suite of systems.

We're all different and react to the way systems work on a different level.

Laurens: That's right. That's why you must create systems that work for you. You won't be successful if you just try to copy my systems because they come with my ideas.

You'll either stop trading when eventually your system will have a period when it's just not working, or you will try to modify it while trading it live. This will lead to a lot of frustration and anxiety.

Alexei: Yes, since I was your student, originally, I thought to myself, like I'd assume most people do: why can't I just copy your systems and be happy with that? You're the expert after all, and wouldn't it be more appropriate to copy from an expert instead of for me to invent the system with my limited knowledge?

Then, as I've designed more and more systems, I've also slowly realized I can't be happy and trust a system that I don't fully understand. I'll have all kinds of thoughts and whispers in my head telling me, "Well, Lauren's designed that system, and he doesn't really care what his system does when the market is going up."

Laurens: That's right. I personally don't really compare my Suite of Systems to the market, but I do know that a lot of people find it useful to compare. This is probably because banks and hedge funds typically compare it to a certain benchmark to justify how they outperform it. But I don't care. All I care about is my suite of systems is making money where I expect it to.

That's why I have my ideas on what I want to tolerate from the risk perspective and what my returns are for my suite in the long run. The older I get, the more I concentrate on protecting my downside [drawdowns].

Alexei: Absolutely! I still don't like to see my systems go down when the market is rallying but I hear you.

Laurens: See, and that's exactly what you need to do for yourself. You need to define your objectives and what you really need while developing your suite of systems.

Alexei: Agreed. Some people love Mean Reversions and day trading, some hate them. Some can only accept Long-Term Trend Following and some can't stand it. Pretty much every single student we have has different ideas and needs. The only main unifying side of it all is they all agree that systematic trading is much easier to handle and better than discretionary trading.

Laurens: That's true. That's why I've started trading way back the way I do now is because I couldn't stand to do it on the discretionary basis.

I've won a lot and then lost it all as I've sabotaged myself.

I've stared at the screen all day, and then realized it leads to a lot of stress, which leads to a lot of bad decisions.

That was why I wrote that *30-Minute Stock Trader* book in the first place. I wanted people to know what I know – you don't have to spend a lot of time in front of the screen to be a professional trader and you can have financial freedom too at the same time.

Alexei: That's true beyond truth. I'm a living proof of this myself because that's how I've stepped on my path to be a systematic trader and the only regret that I have is: why didn't you write this book sooner and I didn't discover it ten years earlier?

Laurens: I wish I knew it earlier for myself as well and thank God that my close friend asked me to write this book as I didn't realize how valuable it could be to other people.

Alexei: Oh well, at least this is not a secret anymore for the world and we can both share this knowledge with others.

CHAPTER 10

Next Steps

The World Of Possibilities

If you have an open mind and are curious about what else you can do with this, then a world of possibilities awaits you!

You know what rules can do and how to use them. You know that it can be flexible for almost any situation.

Yes, I'm not kidding. It's true. It doesn't matter what your current situation is. You can create your own systems and get the benefits using a systematic approach.

- If you have an IRA account and can't trade often and you'd rather trade using mutual funds or maybe ETFs, then you can create a set of systems to handle your mutual funds and ETFs. It would be better than having no rules at all or having some vague ideas on when to buy and when to sell your positions.
- If you can't short stocks because you're in your IRA again, then you can create a Long Only Suite of Systems

and possibly use inverted ETFs to substitute your short positions wherever it makes sense.

- If you don't want to hold positions overnight because it doesn't let you sleep, then you can create a Suite of Systems with day trading versions only.
- If, on the other hand, you hate fast-paced day trading systems and a lot of churns in your suite and want to just have things for the long haul, then you can create a Suite of Systems with LTTF Longs only with some hedge protection.

The combinations of what you can create are literally endless.

Take Action – The Time Is Now

When I talk to my friends, they know how passionate I am about this. Some of them are asking for advice, and some are just afraid to take the initiative into their own hands.

They might ask as an example, "Alexei, what do you think is going to happen if the debt ceiling isn't raised?" My answer is, "How would I really know?" I have an opinion, but does it really matter what I think? My systems were designed to deal with different market conditions regardless of my opinion for a reason. A lot of times my opinion is just plain wrong but am I glad that my systems did what they did!

Let me tell you my little story.

I live in the suburbs of Chicago. It's a nice quiet and green village with a lot of trees, single-family homes, and quite a few retention ponds.

Before I moved in here, I knew that retention ponds are used to collect water if there is a lot of rain and the storm drains can't keep up with it.

What I didn't realize is that typically they put in a lot of retention ponds for a very good reason: either storm drains are narrow, or the land is so flat that water doesn't have any place to go, or both. Turns out we have a pretty flat land here.

All is good. Life goes on. Rain comes and goes. Sun comes and goes. Seasons come and go. It's a Midwestern life, not too far from Lake Michigan.

You get used to the rhythm, and you start taking some things for granted. You don't notice anything until your sump pump stops working in your basement. When the sump pump stops working, and if you don't have a backup pump, then your basement floods, which is something you really don't want to have happen.

I was getting ready to leave for an international business trip. I put all the clothing I'm going to need on my bed – check; getting all my toiletries – check; now I need to get my luggage to put it all in. I'll be leaving early in the morning and it's 9 p.m. already. Oh, yes, and it's in my basement. Let me go and get it.

I pass through the kitchen to the basement door. It's dark down there, so I turn on the light and the first thing I see is... water at the bottom of the stairs! Stuff is floating nicely on the surface, like mini-boats on the lake; some toys from my kids were sitting in cartons that were forgotten as the kids grew up; some pieces of paper from God knows what; oh, and look at that, I see my old laptop is quietly submerged and playing a submarine game with me. The water is not deep, about four-to-six inches, but it's enough to be an unpleasant surprise to discover right before my flight the next morning.

So, I spent the next three hours draining it, cleaning my basement, and trying to dry it. I also have to take out all the wet rugs, which seem to weigh a ton each, up the stairs into my garage. I, of course, have to call the plumber for the emergency service. (They charge you a lot more for that!)

What a fun evening to have all the while I'm thinking about that stupid backup sump pump that I knew went out half a year before. What were the chances that both of sump pumps would go out within six months of each other? You'd probably say almost zero percent and yet, here we are with the problem at hand.

I should've fixed that pump. I knew that we live in an area where we must have working pumps.

I knew that I had that problem.

I was waiting for a good time to do it, always postponing it, as some more important things would find their way into my life.

The good times never came until the disaster hit.

Well, don't repeat my mistakes. Don't wait for "the good time to come"; do it now and don't look back!

You know you can do it. You know it can be done, so why don't you take things into your own hands and act now?

People who act now always reap the benefits!

APPENDIX A

My Favorite Tools To Use

Price Data Provider

Here is my favorite data provider:

- Norgate Data: https://norgatedata.com/

These guys are doing an outstanding job not only with quality data and the breadth of it for different instruments and angles but also with the way they work.

What I mean is I can quickly access data for all the stocks, futures, economic data, current fundamentals, currency pairs, all the indexes (world and US), and all kinds of additional things that you might not even know exist.

They have a very robust and quick interface that is used for connecting our software package to extract data dynamically and seamlessly on the fly to use it for backtesting and order generation.

In all the tests in the book, I've used our QuantumX software which connects to Norgate via a direct connection. This makes it quick and easy to work with as no extra steps are required to convert data from one format to another. Although, Norgate is capable of that too.

Here is a sample interface of Norgate Updater application as of this writing:

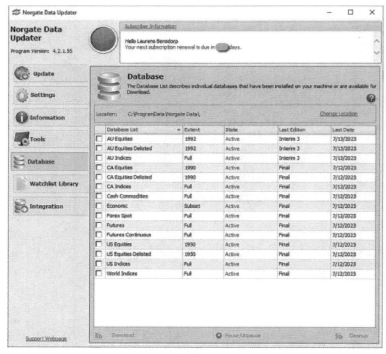

Figure 11.1: Norgate Updater application.

As you can see, it has all kinds of data sources I can hook up to and use for backtesting and order generation.

Also, they have additional dynamically created values and watch lists that could be very useful for system development.

For example, if I need to see what the current US Prime Rate is and all its historical values, I can just view it and use it in my calculations:

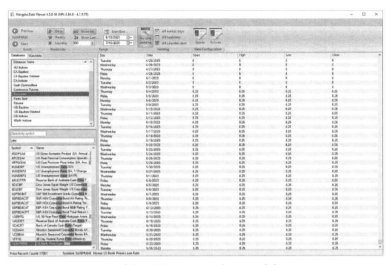

Figure 11.2: Example of the US Prime Rate historical data.

I can also use this for my backtesting if I desire, and I have an indicator that I can use.

There are other things that are quite relevant for the "ideas" that I have to formulate my systems. For example, if I need to know what VIX (fear index) is doing, I can use that index to either get into a position or exit from the positions. This is used for a Market Price filter kind of approach.

I can also dig into any value, something like how many stocks were trending above their 200-day SMA from a specific index or an exchange. It's all very powerful information that is right at the fingertips for you to access and use.

Charting Software

I actually don't use software for it, but rather use a couple of well-known websites:

- TradingView.com: https://www.tradingview.com/
- Yahoo! Finance: https://finance.yahoo.com/

These two are my favorites, and obviously, there are a lot more out there to use.

My main goal for using these tools is to visually see how a stock is behaving for me to come up with the idea for my system.

Remember how we've created our MR Long system with the pullback to EMA (five or nine days)? That's exactly how I work with it. I've looked at the charts, found a common pattern that I see a lot. Then I try to create these as my rules for the system and test it using the backtesting software package (QuantumX application, detailed below).

I personally prefer TradingView.com more than Yahoo! Finance as it's easier to use in some cases, but if I need to quickly view something up along with fundamentals and other information, I'll use Yahoo! Finance for that. Everything is available there for quick access.

Feel free to use something else; just model the approach of how to formulate your idea and translate it into the testable and actionable system rules.

Backtesting Software

In all of the tests, I've used software developed using our main approach in mind. It's called the QuantumX application and it's only available to our students, which you can check out on our website:

https://www.TradingSystems.com

I'm the lead developer of this application, and it was created for the key reason that I couldn't find anything good and reliable enough for me to use out there for the non-correlated approach that I keep mentioning throughout this book.

It all started from using another software package, but it was working so slowly that it was taking 15 minutes for a very simple single test and four hours for the suite of 20 systems.

I used to run it and just sit and read a book for a single test, then look at the results and do it again, and again. It was excruciatingly slow. So, I decided to come up with software as a helper to speed things up.

Then, six months later, it became an application full of features that you can see now in our demo videos and all the screenshots in this book.

All of our students and former students switched to it and use it to run their suites of systems live and for system development.

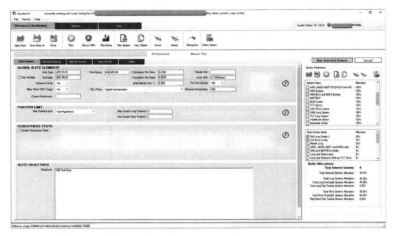

Figure 11.3: Suite Global Parameters screenshot.

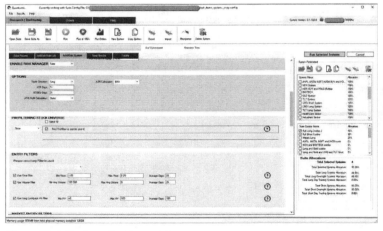

Figure 11.4: System development screen.

200

Below are sample screenshots of the current version of the software, where I can design all the systems (all the examples used in this book are created using this exact software).

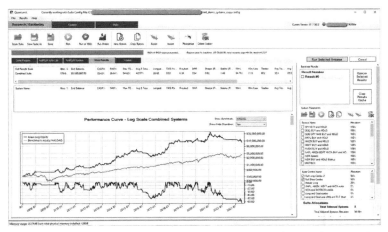

Figure 11.5: LTTF Long Healthcare Sector system results as of writing this book.

In addition to the performance curve shown in Figure 11.5, there are other statistics available for all the backtested results. These include Exposure Charts, Orders Charts, Trades Charts, Monthly and Yearly Returns, among others.

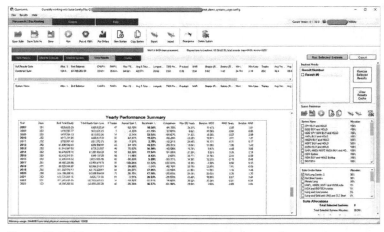

Figure 11.6: Other statistics available for the same results.

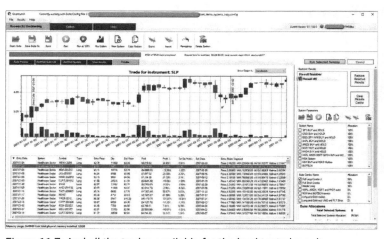

Figure 11.7: And all the trades available for the backtested results.

Also, we can see all the current positions and any new orders that we need to issue for today.

Everything is ready for testing and trading stocks live.

The software was designed as a point-and-click approach to create systems based on your ideas without the need to code any scripting language. It's meant for ease of use for a regular curious person who wants to learn and use our approach of non-correlated systems.

You can see how it works in our demo at https://www. TradingSystems.com

ABOUT THE AUTHOR

Alexei Rudometkin is the Chief Technology Officer and lead software architect for Trading Mastery School. He is the creator of the "QuantumX" trading platform, which enables traders to run dozens of non-correlated trading systems simultaneously and is 90% faster than previous platforms.

Alexei began his career designing technical diagnostic plans for nuclear operations, which included the development of statistical models to detect the most minute variations in operational standards. He later developed neural networking applications for search engines and was an active participant in the development of code for visual mapping and AI-based self-organizing relationships for rapid, relevant online searches. Alexei has also been a leader in the application of artificial intelligence for unmanned aerial vehicles.

Alexei is a native of Obninsk, a city close to Moscow, and a graduate of the prestigious Obninsk Institute of Atomic Energy, a branch of the Moscow Physics University, where he earned a master's degree in Nuclear Science. He moved to the United States in 1998 and received his citizenship in 2010.

Alexei is married with two daughters and lives in Chicago. He's a passionate athlete and enjoys grilling fine steaks from the best cattle around the world.

FREE OFFER

Systematic Trading isn't just a strategy—it's a mindset, a discipline, and a path to financial independence. By now, you've gained insights into how rules-based trading can remove emotion, improve consistency, and help you navigate the markets with confidence.

But knowledge alone isn't enough—**execution is key**. The markets reward those who take action, refine their strategies, and remain committed to continuous learning.

That's why I created the **Free Course**, designed to reinforce what you've learned and help you apply these principles in a structured way. If you haven't already, be sure to claim your access here:

https://www.TradingSystems.com/get-my-free-course

Thank you for joining me on this journey. Stay disciplined, stay systematic, and most importantly—stay in the game.

Wishing you success in your trading and beyond!

Made in the USA
Columbia, SC
21 February 2025

54225664R00113